Morningside Center for Teaching Social Responsibility

THE 4Rs™ TEACHING GUIDE 3
Reading, Writing, Respect & Resolution

Maxine Phillips & Tom Roderick

The 4Rs™ (Reading, Writing, Respect & Resolution)
A Teaching Guide, Grade 3
Principal Writers: Maxine Phillips & Tom Roderick
Literacy Consultant: Barbara Danish
Editing & Design: Leslie Dennis

New edition
Copyright © 2015 by Morningside Center for Teaching Social Responsibility
Earlier editions 2012, 2007, 2001
All rights reserved.
Educators have permission to copy handouts for classroom use.

ISBN-13: 978-1-931630-73-3
ISBN-13: 978-1-931630-13-9 (Learning Kit / Grade 3)

Published by Morningside Center for Teaching Social Responsibility
475 Riverside Drive, Suite 550, New York, NY 10115
T: 212 870 3318 x38 / F: 212 870 2464
Website: www.morningsidecenter.org / Contact: LDennis@morningsidecenter.org

Grade 3

Acknowledgments

The 4Rs has been the work of many hands, minds, and hearts. We first express our gratitude to the following people, organizations, agencies, and institutions that helped us create and launch The 4Rs:

- The working group of teachers from New York City's Community School District 15 who, in a series of meetings during the 1998-99 school year, helped us decide on the themes the curriculum would address and develop an overall plan: Sara Barnes, Paula Beck, Mary Ellen Bosch, Sheila Brooks, Bea Byrd, Alexa Fila, Christina Fuentes, Millie Fulford, Beth Handman, Linda Harris, Catherine Kelly, Lorrie Mann, and Joel Moss.

- The teachers who piloted the draft units during the 1999-2000 school year and gave us their feedback: Chris Bellman, Alison Brackman, Susan Butler, Sarah Button, Alev Dervish, Eileen Eiger, Linda Harris, Julio Jimenez, Cathy Kelly, Lorrie Mann, Denise McCarthy, Joel Moss, Ellen Neipris, Mary Beth Palmer, Donna Pasquariello, Pascale Pradel, Debra Sit, and Kim Tulloch.

- Frank DeStefano, Superintendent of CSD 15, and Wilfredo Laboy, Assistant Superintendent, who supported the project from the beginning and made it possible for teachers to participate.

- Principals of the schools where teachers piloted the units: Mary Manti, Principal, P.S. 15; Yvette Aguirre, Principal, P.S. 24; Linda Leff, Principal, P.S. 58; Josephine Santiago, Principal, P.S. 169; Howard Wholl, Principal, P.S. 230; Judi Aronson, Principal, P.S. 261; Liz Phillips, Principal, P.S. 321.

- Morningside Center (then called Educators for Social Responsibility Metropolitan Area/ESR Metro) staff members: Barbara Barnes, Lillian Castro, Leslie Dennis, Larry Garvin, Laura McClure, Nino Nannarone, Mary Schreiber, Heather Smith, and Jeanette Toomer.

- Barbara Danish, our literacy consultant, who emphasized the importance of writing as a tool for thinking.

- People whose work in the field of conflict resolution/social and emotional learning contributed to our thinking about the 4Rs: Sheila Alson, Larry Dieringer, William Kreidler, Linda Lantieri, Priscilla Prutzman, Jinnie Spiegler, Sandy Whittal, and the staff of the New York City Board of Education Office of the Resolving Conflict Creatively Program: Donna Connelly, Mariana Gaston, Ellen Icolari, Hannah Kirschner, Angela Morgan, Debra Schaller-Demers, Lina Sullivan, Jim Tobin, Manny Verdi.

- Our Foundation and Corporate Supporters: Booth Ferris Foundation, Chase Bank, Fund for the City of New York, J.P. Morgan Charitable Trust, Met Life Foundation, Overbrook Foundation, The Philip and Lynn Straus Foundation, The Pinkerton Foundation.

Second, we thank the following people, organizations, agencies, and institutions that, believing in The 4Rs, have helped us develop, sustain, and expand the program:

- The thousands of teachers who have studied the teaching guides and taught the curriculum to their students.
- Principals who have championed The 4Rs in their schools and beyond, especially Christina Fuentes, P.S. 24, Brooklyn; David Cintron, P.S. 214, The Bronx; Lisa Manfredonia, P.S. 62, The Bronx; Maria Nunziata, P.S. 130, Brooklyn: Roberta Davenport, P.S. 307, Brooklyn; and Rose Dubitsky, P.S 24, Brooklyn.
- Jenni Turner, early childhood teacher, who advised us in writing The 4Rs Teaching Guide for Pre-k.

- Audrey Major and Janice Marie Johnson, Morningside Center staff members, who helped shape The 4Rs for Middle School.
- Jill Merolla, Supervisor of Community Outreach and Grant Development for the Warren City Schools, who championed The 4Rs, a key component of Warren's SEL Skills for Life Program.
- The research team that conducted the gold-standard (randomized control) study of The 4Rs Program: Dr. J. Lawrence Aber, New York University, Dr. Joshua Brown, Fordham University, and Dr. Stephanie Jones, Harvard University.
- The research team for Goal 2 4Rs+My Teaching Partner (MTP) Project: Dr. Joshua Brown, Fordham University; Drs. Jason Downer and Megan Stuhlman, University of Virginia; Dr. Stephanie Jones, Harvard University.
- The research team for the federally funded Goal 3 randomized control trial of the 4Rs + My Teaching Partner Project: Dr. Joshua Brown, Fordham University; and Drs. Jason Downer and Megan Stuhlman, University of Virginia.
- Suzanne Bouffard, who wrote a great article about The 4Rs-MTP Project for the New York Tiimes.
- Our friends at the Collaborative for Academic, Social, and Emotional Learning (CASEL), especially Roger Weissberg and the late Mary Utne O'Brien.
- My dear long-time colleague Linda Lantieri, Director, Inner Resilience Program, from whom we have learned much that has strengthened all of Morningside Center's work, including The 4Rs.
- Susan Fountain, who is helping us highlight and strengthen the aspects of The 4Rs that helps students pause, focus, and pay attention to what is happening in the present moment.
- Those of our staff developers who have trained and coached teachers in The 4Rs: Audrey Major, Ava Daniel, Mariana Gaston, Emma Gonzalez, Janice Marie Johnson, Javier Diaz, Joseph McCarthy, Joyce Griffen, Kristin Page Stuart, Marieke van Woerkom,
- Carolina Kroon, photographer and videographer, who captured many images and videos of 4Rs activities over the years.
- Leslie Dennis, Morningside Center Program Associate, who designed The 4Rs Teaching Guides and Learning Kits and handles production and shipping of the guides and kits with loving and much appreciated attention to detail.
- The authors and illustrators of the wonderful children's books that introduce The 4Rs units.
- Connie Cuttle who has championed Morningside Center's work, including The 4Rs, as Director of Professional Development, the Office of Safety and Youth Development, New York City Department of Education.
- Our funders: Jean and Louis Dreyfus Foundation, Keith and Miller Foundation, Marianne Montero, New York City Department of Education, New York Community Trust, Novo Foundation, Philip and Lynn Straus Foundation, The Pinkerton Foundation, Tiger Foundation, U.S. Department of Education, U.S. Department of Education, Institute of Education Sciences, WT Grant Foundation.
- Maxine Phillips, my wife and co-author, whose appreciation for high-quality children's literature and her knack for finding just the right book to launch each unit have immeasurably enriched The 4Rs.

Tom Roderick
Executive Director
Morningside Center for Teaching Social Responsibility
August 2015

Grade 3

Contents

Acknowledgments iii

Table of Contents v

Introduction vii

Tips for Teachers xiii

4Rs Curriculum Themes and Books xvii

Unit 1: Building Community / Stone Soup 1
Introduction / In this unit 2
About the book 4
Book Talk 5
Applied Learning 7
Related Books 14
Handouts 15

Unit 2: Feelings / JoJo's Flying Side Kick 17
Introduction / In this unit 18
About the book 20
Book Talk 21
Applied Learning 23
Related Books 40
Handouts 41

Unit 3: Listening / The Pain and the Great One 45
Introduction / In this unit 46
About the book 48
Book Talk 49
Applied Learning 52
Related Books 62

Unit 4: Assertiveness / Hank Aaron: Brave in Every Way 63
Introduction / In this unit 64
About the book 66
Book Talk 68
Applied Learning 70
Related Books 80
Handouts 81

Unit 5: Problem Solving / Old Henry 83
Introduction / In this unit 84
About the book 86
Book Talk 87
Applied Learning 89
Related Books 97
Handouts 98

Unit 6: Diversity /Countering Bullying / One 101
Introduction / In this unit 102
About the book 105
Book Talk 106
Applied Learning 108
Related Books 120
Handouts 121

Unit 7: Making a Difference / Baseball Saved Us 123
Introduction / In this unit 124
About the book 126
Book Talk 128
Applied Learning 130
Related Books 137
Handouts 138

Bibliography 140

Index
Activities, Closings, Gatherings, & Handouts 141

Grade 3

Introduction

Welcome to The 4Rs!

You are about to embark on an adventure with your students than can transform your classroom, their lives, and perhaps your own. The 4Rs™ (Reading, Writing, Respect, and Resolution) is a unique program that combines excellent children's literature with social and emotional skill-building. Research has shown that when it is adopted school wide it has measurable impact on both classroom atmosphere and students' social, emotional, and cognitive development. As students learn the skills they need to deal constructively with their peers and to manage their own emotions, they are able to focus more easily on academics.

A program of Morningside Center for Teaching Social Responsibility, The 4Rs integrates social and emotional learning (SEL) and language arts from pre-kindergarten to 8th grade. Through the program, Morningside Center provides training and classroom coaching to prepare teachers to teach weekly lessons based on The 4Rs curriculum.

The 4Rs for pre-k to 5th grade uses high-quality children's literature and engaging interactive activities to develop students' skills and understanding in seven areas: building community, understanding and handling feelings, listening, assertiveness, problem-solving, dealing well with diversity, and cooperation. The 4Rs curriculum is grade-specific: Each grade has its own teaching guide, books, and age-appropriate activities.

Each 4Rs unit begins with a Read-aloud of a children's book, carefully chosen for its high literary quality and relevance to the theme. Next is Book Talk — discussion, writing, and role-play to deepen students' understanding of the book and connect it to their lives. Then comes Applied Learning — skills practice related to the theme.

By highlighting universal themes of feelings, relationships, conflict, and community, the 4Rs curriculum adds meaning and depth to literacy instruction. Since reading and writing are excellent tools for exploring social and emotion themes, The 4Rs enriches SEL instruction as well.

The 4Rs engages parents through "4Rs Family Connections," which has two parts:
- activities children do at home with their parents and

- workshops that bring parents together to explore how social and emotional skills can strengthen their relationships with their children.

The 4Rs program has been rigorously studied, thanks to a grant from the U. S. Department of Education.[1] A gold-standard study by top researchers at New York University and Fordham University tracked the development of children in nine New York City elementary schools that implemented the program compared with the development of children in nine control schools. Compared with children in the control schools, children in the 4Rs schools were less hyperactive, less aggressive, and saw their social world as less hostile. They showed fewer symptoms of depression and were more likely to resolve interpersonal problems competently.

What's more, during the first year children judged to be at greatest behavioral risk by their teachers had better attendance than their counterparts in the control schools and made better academic progress as rated by teachers. By the second year, they were also doing better on standardized tests.

At the end of the first year, independent ("blind") observers assessed the quality of classroom climate in all third-grade classrooms in the 18 schools using a research-based observational instrument called the Classroom Assessment Scoring System (CLASS). These observations showed significantly higher levels of overall classroom quality among classrooms in the 4Rs schools compared to classrooms in the control schools. Specifically, classrooms in 4Rs schools had significantly higher levels of emotional and instructional support compared to classrooms in control schools. Other research has shown a strong correlation between higher levels on the CLASS and more positive social and emotional development and higher academic achievement.

The 4Rs is closely aligned with the national standards set by CASEL (Collaborative for Academic, Social, and Emotional Learning): The 4Rs Program received CASEL's highest ratings in its Guide to Effective SEL Programs (pre-k-5). The 4Rs is also included in the federal Substance Abuse and Mental Health Services Administration's National Registry of Evidence-Based Programs and Practices.

Taken together, the ratings and research above demonstrate that The 4Rs Program is an evidence-based program that should be available to schools everywhere.

---

[1] Jones, S. M., Brown, J. L.& Aber, J. L. (2011). Two-year impacts of a universal school-based social-emotional and literacy intervention: An experiment in translational developmental research. *Child Development, 82* (2), 533–554.

Social and Emotional Learning

Morningside Center defines social and emotional learning (SEL) as the process by which we develop our capacity to understand and manage our feelings, relate well to others, deal well with conflict and other life challenges, make good decisions, and take responsibility for improving our communities – from the classroom to the world.

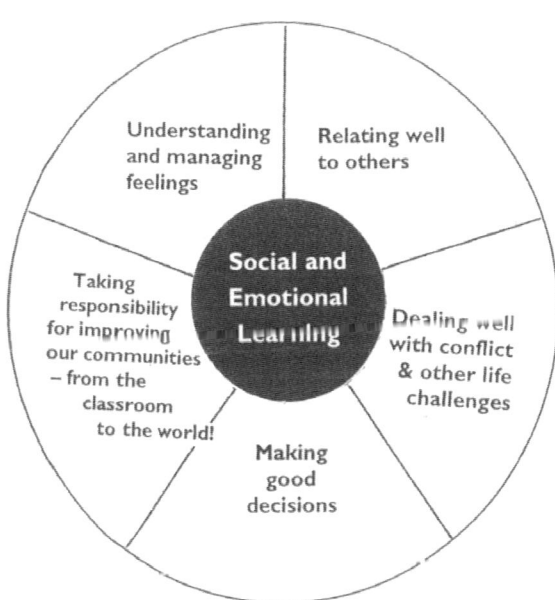

Social and Emotional Learning
Five Competencies

Social and Emotional Learning is the process by which we develop our capacity to
1) understand & manage our feelings;
2) relate well to others;
3) deal well with conflict & other life challenges;
4) make good decisions; *and*
5) take responsibility for improving our communities – from the classroom to the world!

Each of these competencies is made up of a number of skills. For example, ***Understanding and managing our feelings*** involves, among other things, the ability to be aware of and name our feelings, an understanding of the physical cues to emotions, insight into what triggers certain emotions, and the ability to express emotions appropriately and constructively.

The ability to relate well to others requires the ability to read the emotions of others, empathize, listen actively, and communicate assertively. It also includes the capacity to understand similarities and differences; to work respectfully across gender, race, ethnic, religious, economic, ability, and other types of differences; and to examine one's own assumptions and stereotypes.

Dealing well with conflict and other life challenges involves emotional self-management, effective listening and communication skills, and an understanding that what one asks for in conflict and what one really needs may not be the same. It also includes the ability to come up with alternative solutions to conflicts, skill in evaluating possible solutions, and a commitment to solving problems in a way that meets the real needs of all parties.

Making good decisions requires awareness of the motivations behind our choices; engages students' ability to assess the consequences of those choices; encourages students to think about how decisions they take will affect them, others, and the larger community; and helps students look back at decisions made and assess their impact.

Taking responsibility for improving our communities harnesses the skills described above in the service of social justice. It entails an understanding of what justice means and the ability to identify situations of injustice, as well as familiarity with the actions of those who have made a difference in our society. It also requires that students see themselves as capable of taking responsible action and are willing to take meaningful action, both individually and with others.

Taking time to slow down and focus on these skills is something that may be new to your students. Yet the ability to step back and notice our feelings and thoughts, as well as how we are interacting with others, is foundational to developing and using social and emotional competencies. Throughout the 4Rs curriculum, there are activities that help students to pay attention to their sensory experiences, thoughts, and emotions in the present moment. These activities may

> **The seven units in The 4Rs are designed to support the development of these SEL competencies:**
>
> **Unit 1, Community Building**, helps students build a sense of caring and connection in their classrooms.
>
> **Unit 2, Feelings**, heightens students' awareness of their own emotions, and those of others, while providing practical strategies for managing strong emotions like anger.
>
> **Unit 3, Listening**, fosters skills that enable students to understand where others are coming from, learn from them, and empathize with them.
>
> **Unit 4, Assertiveness**, is about being strong but not mean in expressing one's needs and in standing up for what one thinks is right
>
> **Unit 5: Problem Solving**, shows how to resolve issues and handle conflicts in ways that meet the priority needs of both parties.
>
> **Unit 6, Diversity**, cultivates a sense of one's own identity, respect for differences, and commitment to standing up to bullying.
>
> **Unit 7, Making a Difference**, looks how others have brought about change, with the goal of creating positive change in the classroom, school, local community, and beyond.

involve simply noticing their breathing, attending to sounds, or being more aware of their physical movements. Building this kind of awareness encourages students to pause, notice what is happening inside and outside themselves, and respond thoughtfully rather than react automatically. Research suggests that when these types of activities are used regularly, they may help students feel more centered, manage their emotions more effectively, and increase both attention and social-emotional competency.[2]

The impact of SEL programs

In schools where SEL is well-implemented, students develop their social and emotional competencies; become partners with adults in creating vibrant learning communities; and learn to care about and respect other people, including those who are different or who live far away.

A growing body of research shows that students in high quality SEL programs
- show improved social and emotional skills and behavior;
- decrease their classroom misbehavior and aggression;
- increase positive attitudes about themselves, others and school;
- improve their attendance
- reduce their anxiety and depression;
- are less like to be suspended;
- gain in achievement test scores and have better grades.

A new vision for education

Morningside Center understands SEL as a set of attitudes, practices, and policies that are fully integrated into the life and culture of the school, rather than as an add-on "program." SEL can provide a rich vision of education and a basis for reflecting on everything that goes on in a school. By asking how school policies and practices are affecting students' social and emotional development, SEL can be a powerful lever for school improvement. By building caring and connections, SEL also lays a solid foundation for social responsibility, not only toward friends and family but toward ever-widening circles of community.

---

[2] Greenberg, M. T. & Harris, A. R. (2012). Nurturing mindfulness in children and youth: Current state of research. *Child Development Perspectives, 6* (2), 161-166.

Morningside Center for Teaching Social Responsibility

Morningside Center works hand in hand with educators to help young people develop the values, personal qualities, and skills they need to thrive and contribute to their communities — from the classroom to the world.

Since our founding in 1982, Morningside Center has developed an array of programs to engage young people in learning essential social and emotional skills and to support educators in making their schools productive and respectful. Over the years our programs have reached hundreds of schools, tens of thousands of educators, and hundreds of thousands of students, grades pre-k - 12, in New York City and beyond.

Major scientific studies have found that our programs have a significant positive impact on students' behavior, their social and emotional competency, their academic performance, and on the classroom climate for learning. The Collaborative for Academic, Social & Emotional Learning (CASEL) has selected two of our programs (The 4Rs and Resolving Conflict Creatively) as among the nation's top 23 SEL programs.

We are part of a nationwide movement to make high-quality, research-validated social and emotional learning an integral part of every child's education.

For more information visit our website at www.morningsidecenter.org.

Tom Roderick
Executive Director
August 2015

Tips for Teachers: Getting the most from The 4Rs™

1. **Do at least one lesson a week throughout the school year.** Consistency is the key to effectiveness. This means making The 4Rs a priority, not an optional activity you do if time permits. It means continuing to teach The 4Rs even when standardized tests are looming. In fact, you can use 4Rs ideas and skills to help your students handle their feelings about the tests and lower their stress level so that they can improve their performance.

2. **Choose prime time at the same time each week for your 4Rs lessons.** Your week will go better if your 4Rs lesson is first thing Monday morning (or Tuesday morning if Monday is a holiday). Avoid Friday afternoons! In fact, The 4Rs is most successful when all classroom teachers are teaching The 4Rs at the same time each week. During that time, the entire staff of the school is doing 4Rs, with out-of-classroom staff (guidance counselors and social workers, for example) assisting classroom teachers and principals and assistant principals visiting classrooms to observe and publicly acknowledge good work by students and teachers.

3. **Spend about five weeks per unit.** Because there are seven units, it will take about 35 weeks to teach the entire curriculum. Each unit consists of a Read-aloud, Book Talk, and (with a few exceptions) three Applied Learning lessons in the workshop format (see below). Do the Read-aloud and Book Talk in Week 1 and the Applied Learning lessons in Weeks 2, 3, and 4. Use Week 5 to engage the students in a project related to the unit, to reinforce a skill with which the students need more practice, to revisit the Read-aloud for the unit, and/or read them another book on the theme.

4. **Meet weekly with colleagues to share experiences and ideas** and do problem solving when challenges arise. At a minimum The 4Rs should be on the agenda of grade meetings each week. In addition, interested teachers may want to set up a weekly conversation about the curriculum over lunch.

5. **Teach the curriculum in the sequence provided.** Dealing well with feelings, being a good listener, and being assertive (strong, not mean) lay the foundation for effective problem solving, for cultural sharing and standing up to bullying, and for making a difference. Of course, if a teachable moment arises, you can take the opportunity to bring in an idea or skill from a later or earlier unit. But keep your main focus on the unit at hand.

6. **Use the workshop format for the Applied Learning lessons.** The lessons are carefully designed to provide an optimal context for learning. The full lesson or workshop has a much greater impact than doing the activities out-of-context.

The <u>Gathering</u> helps students leave behind any baggage they're carrying from other parts of their day and directs their attention to "4Rs Time." <u>Checking the Agenda</u> gives students some ownership over this part of their day. The core activities address the workshop's key objectives. The <u>Evaluation</u> gives you feedback on students' perceptions of the lesson. The <u>Closing</u> ends the workshop on a positive note and gives the message that "4Rs Time" is over for the day.

7. **Call the time you set aside for 4Rs instruction "4Rs Time."** Make sure students know what the 4Rs stand for. Of course, as The 4Rs takes root in your classroom, you'll be applying 4Rs ideas and skills throughout the day. But it's important that "4Rs Time" has its own identity as a special time to focus attention on social and emotional learning—in the same way that reading goes on throughout the day but there's the "literacy block" when attention is focused on literacy.

8. **"4Rs Time" works best when the students sit in a circle.** Have the students sit in a circle on the rug. Or, if the students will be sitting in chairs, have them move furniture and arrange their chairs, as necessary. You can turn this task into a cooperative game by asking them to do this in silence and as quickly as possible. Time them and post the result, and next time see if they beat their best time so far.

9. **Use a talking piece—with discretion.** Morningside Center recommends using a talking piece as part of a structured "circle" process for fostering deep communication when you want everyone's voice to be heard by everyone else in your class. The students are sitting in a circle with no obstructions in the middle. The talking piece is passed around the circle in order from one student to the next. In this way, each member of the circle is invited to speak, and they know when their turn is coming up. They can pass if they want to. When a student is holding the talking piece, it's that student's turn to talk and enjoy the full attention of the group. No one is allowed to go out of turn—to interrupt, ask a question, or make a comment. All have to wait until the talking piece comes around to them. You don't have time to go through this process for everything you want your students to share. For brainstorming, a brief discussion, or calling on a couple of students to speak after a pair-share, a talking piece might be cumbersome. Feel free to integrate a circle with talking piece into The 4Rs when you want to slow things down a bit and take the time to hear everybody's thinking.

10. **Foster SEL all day every day by**
    - modeling the skills you are teaching your students
    - integrating 4Rs ideas, skills, and activities into other areas of the curriculum
    - taking advantage of teachable moments, and

- engaging your students in special projects (for example, creating posters on SEL themes to display around the school or creating skits to perform for other classes or for parents).

11. **Model active listening with your students.** Your teaching of The 4Rs curriculum will be most successful if students feel comfortable sharing their experiences and their thinking. Listen without judgment, use active listening techniques (like paraphrasing) to draw out their thinking, and encourage them to share their points of view with you and each other in respectful ways. If you feel the need to challenge a student's ideas or correct misinformation, do so gently and respectfully and, as much as possible, by asking questions that complicate the student's thinking.

12. **Set aside a few minutes each day for silence.** The school day is hectic and stressful for students and teachers. It's useful to build in time each day for a few minutes of silence. During this time the lights are off. No writing, drawing, or reading. Just sitting. Ask students to put their hands on their knees. They can close their eyes if they want. Tell them that they can let their minds use the silence as they wish. Or you can suggest ways they might use the silence. For example,
    - practice abdominal breathing (introduced in Unit 2)
    - simply pay attention to your breathing
    - pay attention to sounds you hear
    - in your mind, take yourself to a peaceful place
    - recall a time you had fun
    - recall something you like to do

    a. After the time of silence, ask for a couple of volunteers to share where their minds went during the time. Make time for silence each day at the same time. You might carve out a few minutes for silence when the students come back from lunch and recess and/or at the beginning of the day. Throughout the curriculum we suggest times when teachers might ask students to pause and pay attention to what is happening inside (their sensations, images, feelings, thoughts) and outside (sounds, sights, the feelings and behavior of others). The ability to pause and pay attention to what's happening in the moment is a key social and emotional skill that promotes self-awareness and self-management.

    b. A few minutes of silence at strategic times during the day will pay off in a calmer, more focused class. And you'll be developing in your students a habit and skill that will serve them well throughout their lives.

    c. Be sure to take this opportunity to enjoy a couple of minutes of silence yourself!

13. **Consider having your students keep a 4Rs/SEL journal.** Writing (drawing for younger students) is an excellent way to reinforce and consolidate learning. A powerful research-based study technique is to follow the reading of a text by writing about it, perhaps summarizing the main points of an argument and articulating your response. By writing about a text we can test our understanding and identify gaps we can fill by reviewing sections of the text. We enhance our memory of the text. And we exercise our creative- thinking muscles as we fashion our response. That's why we've included writing exercises as part of Book Talk in all units for all grades. A journal enables students to put all of their Book Talk writing in one place. You can also give them a few minutes after each 4Rs lesson to jot down a few thoughts about what they're taking away or how they're planning to use what they've just learned. If a student tries a new skill, s/he might want to write about what happened. Did it bring a positive result? If a student is stuck in a conflict with someone, s/he might want to do some writing to sort it out and imagine some solutions. You can give your students standard journals and encourage them to decorate them. By having students keep journals, you will be introducing them to a habit or practice that can serve them well the rest of their lives.

14. **Class meetings for problem solving are an excellent extension of The 4Rs.** In this kind of class meeting the teacher empowers students, facilitating a process by which they apply the skills they're developing through 4Rs lessons to real-life problems in classroom and school. Introduce class meetings for problem solving after completing Unit 5. By this time your students will have the foundational skills (managing feelings, listening, assertiveness) to be good problem solvers. Also, Unit 5 has a lesson on the ABCDE problem-solving model, an approach that children can easily grasp. A free downloadable copy of Morningside Center's comprehensive guide, *Class Meetings for Problem Solving*, is available by request.

15. **Add your own ideas.** You know your students. Tailor the curriculum to their needs and interests and add your own creative ideas. We've described the recommended activities fully to get you started, but The 4Rs is not a scripted curriculum. Once you get the hang of it, you'll see additional ways to enhance the students' understanding of key ideas and strengthen their skills. Be creative and share your ideas and experiences with your colleagues.

16. **Hang in there, even when the going gets tough.** This is hard work; it can also be immensely gratifying. Gandhi thought of his life as a series of "experiments in nonviolence." He tried things — some worked, some didn't. He learned from his mistakes, kept trying and ended up making a huge difference. In similar fashion, "4Rs Time" provides a great opportunity for you to make a huge difference in the lives of your students.

Grade 3

The 4Rs
Overview of Themes & Books

UNIT	Pre-K	Kindergarten	1st Grade	2nd Grade
Unit 1: Building community	*Hurry, Hurry* by Eve Bunting	*Subway Sparrow* by Leyla Torres	*The Doorbell Rang* by Pat Hutchins	*The Big Orange Splot* by Daniel Manus Pinkwater
Unit 2: Feelings	*Glad Monster, Sad Monster, A Book About Feelings* by Ed Emberley and Anne Miranda	*Mama, Do You Love Me?* by Barbara Joosse Alternate: *When Sophie Gets Angry, Really, Really Angry* by Mollie Bang	*Chrysanthemum* by Kevin Henkes	*We Are Best Friends* by Aliki
Unit 3: Listening	*The Listening Walk* by Paul Showers	*The Hating Book* by Charlotte Zolotow	*Max Found Two Sticks*, written and illustrated by Brian Pinkney	*Angel Child, Dragon Child* by Michele Maria Surat
Unit 4: Assertiveness	*Don't let the Pigeon Drive the Bus* by Mo Willem	*George and Martha: One Fine Day* and *George and Martha: Tons of Fun* by James Marshall	*Daisy Comes Home* by Jan Brett	*The Recess Queen* by Alexis O'Neill, illus. by Laura Huliska-Beith
Unit 5: Problem solving	*The Knight and the Dragon* by Tomie dePaola	*Zinnia and Dot* by Lisa Campbell Ernst	*Owen* by Kevin Henkes	*Luka's Quilt* by Georgia Guback
Unit 6: Diversity	*The Foot Book* by Dr. Seuss	*Stellaluna* by Janell Cannon	*The Ugly Vegetables* by Grace Lin	*Crow Boy* by Taro Yashima
Unit 7: Making a difference	*Click, Clack, MOO, Cows that Type* by Doreen Cronin	*Swimmy* by Leo Lionni	*The Bremen Town Musicians* / retold and illustrated by Ilse Plume	*Wangari's Trees of Peace* by Jeanette Winter

The 4Rs

Overview of Themes & Books

UNIT	3rd Grade	4th Grade	5th Grade
Unit 1: Building community	*Stone Soup* by Marcia Brown	*Alejandro's Gift* by Richard E. Albert	*The Keeping Quilt* by Patricia Polacco
Unit 2: Feelings	*JoJo's Flying Side Kick* by Brian Pinkney	*Sarah, Plain and Tall* by Patricia MacLachlan	*Mysterious Traveler* by Mal Peet & Elspeth Graham (authors), P.J. Lynch (illustrator)
Unit 3: Listening	*The Pain and the Great One* by Judy Blume	*The Other Way to Listen* by Byrd Baylor and Peter Parnall	*Encounter* by Jane Yolen
Unit 4: Assertiveness	*Hank Aaron: Brave in Every Way* by Peter Golenbock	*The Story of Ruby Bridges* by Robert Coles	*Your Move* by Eve Bunting
Unit 5: Problem solving	*Old Henry* by Joan W. Blos	*Chandra's Magic Light: A Story in Nepal,* by Theresa Heine; Judith Gueyfier (illustrator)	*Brothers in Hope* by Mary Williams & R. Gregory Christie
Unit 6: Diversity	*One* by Kathryn Otoshi	*The Hundred Dresses* by Eleanor Estes	*Friends from the Other Side* by Gloria Anzaldua
Unit 7: Making a difference	*Baseball Saved Us* by Ken Mochizuki	*Moses: When Harriet Tubman Led Her People to Freedom* by Carole Boston Weatherford	*Sweet Clara and the Freedom Quilt* by Deborah Hopkinson

3

Unit 1 Theme

Building Community: Developing a Vision

Unit 1 Book Selection

Stone Soup by Marcia Brown

Aladdin Paperbacks, Simon & Schuster, 1997

Activities

- Vision of classroom community
- Good and poor listening
- Think differently
- Put-ups and put-downs
- Have a heart w/ heart story
- Additional Activities

Introduction

Human beings are social and interdependent. We live in and interact with many, many groups, such as family, neighborhood, school, city, state, country, planet, or groups based on faith, work, play, and common identities or interests. However, being part of a group that shares similar characteristics does not necessarily mean that one is part of a community as we use the term here. By community, we mean connection, caring, and solidarity. Such communities do not just happen. They are the result of shared vision and conscious effort. Martin Luther King, Jr. spoke of a dream, of a "beloved community." He articulated a vision that many people share. We all deserve to be part of communities that are safe, fair, caring, respectful, appreciative, and nurturing of our talents. When we speak of building a classroom community, we are talking about creating a group that has those qualities.

Teachers build community through their approach to classroom management. That's the bedrock upon which all else rests. Community building can also occur through the study of literature, which presents visions of community; through discussions in which students and teachers discuss, disagree, and come to various understandings in a supportive context; and through conscious decisions about rights and responsibilities as members of the community.

The dominant U.S. culture is one of the most individualistic in the world. There is a constant tension in our society between the rights of individuals and the rights of groups. These tensions are played out in everyday life as well as in legislatures and courts of law (think of compulsory education, home-schooling, and the right of the Amish to withdraw their children from school at age 14). Existing within the dominant culture are cultures of immigrant and indigenous groups that place more emphasis on community than on individual expression. Literature about different groups will reflect such attitudes and conflicts. Classroom discussion can range over a variety of issues, such as the balance between group rights and individual rights; the oppressiveness of small communities in which everyone knows everybody's business vs. the intimacy of small communities in which everyone cares about each other; the roles people play in communities; the need

> **Community Building in the Classroom Involves**
>
> - Creating a vision of the community you want and setting goals
> - Establishing concrete rules & expectations
> - Enforcing consequences when rules are not followed or expectations not met
> - Establishing and observing group rituals
> - Developing individuals' self-control and interpersonal skills
> - Ongoing communication and problem solving
> - Regular class meetings

for leadership in building community; the variety of communities; and the variety of assumptions or principles that hold communities together.

At the beginning of the school year, teachers usually spend time establishing class rules and routines. This unit intends to support that process. We can think of class rules as guidelines for creating classroom community. The teacher provides good leadership for the community, but guidelines are most effective when developed with the participation of the group.

In this unit students will work with the literature to exercise their imaginations. They will develop their visions of community, learn to listen to each other, and learn to apply the literature to the ongoing process of building community in their classrooms and the world beyond.

> **Rules for a Classroom Community Might Include**
> - Listening well
> - Tolerating disagreements and diverse points of view
> - Respecting each other's bodies
> - Respecting each other's property
> - Respecting each other's feelings

In this unit

	Ideas	Skills
Literacy	• Plot development • How a writer builds tension	• Predicting • Identifying the main idea • Figuring out words in context
Social and Emotional Learning	• Analyzing the problem • Cooperation for short-term goals	• Brainstorming • Asking for help • Working together • Listening • Observing

Stone Soup, by Marcia Brown
Aladdin Paperbacks, Simon & Schuster, 1997

SUMMARY

The wars are over at some unspecified time in the past. Three soldiers are returning to their own country, passing through the French countryside. They have no food or money. They know that local villagers, tired and impoverished by war, will not welcome them. But they decide to ask for help anyway. Meanwhile, the villagers have seen them coming. "Soldiers are always hungry. But we have little enough for ourselves," they say. We do not know if they are particularly greedy or whether they have known other soldiers who took their food and seized sleeping space and money, as soldiers have been known to do. In any case, they are wary and do not want to share anything they have. When the soldiers ask for food and lodging they refuse them. These soldiers, although they have swords, do not try to take anything by force. They confer among themselves and come up with a plan. They tell the villagers that they will have to make stone soup. The villagers are curious. The soldiers ask for a large pot, for water, for fire, for a stone. Then they ask for items to go in the soup, starting with simple requests for salt and pepper, then carrots, cabbage, and on up to meat so that the soup would be fit for a rich man's table, even for the king himself. As the soup becomes richer, so do the villagers, who had presented themselves as on the verge of starvation. Now they offer a roast and side dishes to go with the soup. Soon the whole village is involved and eventually sits down to a feast that they can all enjoy. At the end, when the soldiers ask for a bed, the villagers respond generously, and each man sleeps in one of the finest beds in the village. The next morning, the villagers give them a grand send-off and thank them for the lesson in how to make soup from stones.

COMMENT

This story is rich with possible interpretations and inspiring in its vision. There is another narrower version of it that many students may have read in which the sharing and community-building aspects have been dropped and it becomes a folktale of a poor but clever boy outwitting a wealthy but stingy woman. Versions of this story exist throughout Europe and are part of the folklore of many countries. The version in our curriculum can be seen as an inspiring story of three men weary of war who must use their wits to gain food and lodging and in doing so, teach the villagers how to cooperate with each other. It can also be seen as a story of three clever vagabonds who outwit the selfish townsfolk, who never do catch on to what has happened. The text of the book jacket, for instance, implies an interpretation that we are not making. We can talk about different approaches to the same story.

Through the years people have been inspired by this story to know that that they can make something out of nothing, find strength in combined action, and use their wits to get out of difficult situations. We can look at the different ways the action could have gone, knowing what we do of the behavior of soldiers in war-torn countries, and ways in which the villagers could have responded. We can ask about times in our own lives when we have thought we didn't have enough to share but dug deep and were able to find something. We can agree to disagree about the actual meaning of the story and can look at other folktales and fairy tales that have been changed from their originals. (Note: Almost all U.S.- born children, for instance, will know the Disney version of a fairy tale before encountering its earlier version.) We can talk about storytelling and the power of stories to inspire and teach us. We can engage in our own creative thinking regarding what seem like impossible situations.

Book Talk

READ-ALOUD

Previewing the book

Look at the cover. Ask the students to write down everything they notice about the drawing. What does it tell us about the book? Who do we think the characters will be? What kind of clothing are the characters wearing? Do we know what time frame this might be, what country? Explain the word peasant.

Ask if anyone knows the story. Ask which version. (There is also one in which instead of three soldiers there are brother and sister pigs that are hungry and tired.) Point out that this is a folktale, which means a story told by people over the years that usually teaches something. Every country has its own folktales, and many stories are similar in different countries, but with certain details that mark it as peculiar to a certain country. This story exists in almost every country in Europe in some version. Sometimes it may be only one soldier who comes to a village. Sometimes the villagers really are starving and have very little to contribute, but each gives something.

Look at the first picture, which has no words. Have the students take a couple of minutes to jot down what they notice about the villagers' clothing (child's smock, wooden shoes, the bagpipe, broad hat, pantaloons or culottes of the adult). What kind of streets does this village have? (Cobblestone) Explain that in the days before paved roads there were either dirt streets or cobblestone, and even today, New York City and all of the old cities of Europe have sections with cobblestone streets. The pictures help set the scene as being in another country in another time.

Reading and responding to the book[1]

Read the book slowly, giving the students time to look at the pictures. Stop occasionally and ask the students what is happening, referring to parts of the text when useful.

---

[1] There are different approaches to read-alouds. You may wish to read the book through without stopping at all. You may read through, pausing only when the students ask a question or look puzzled. Or you may choose to do an interactive read-aloud in which you pause from time to time in the reading to point out something, to ask what is happening or what the students think will happen next or what choices the characters could make. Choose the option you prefer. Except in a few cases, the suggestions that follow are based on the assumption that you are reading the book through without pauses except for students' questions. If you decide to do an interactive read-aloud, you can refer to the suggestions in *Deepening students' understanding of the book* for possible stopping places.

After you have finished reading the story, ask the children, what would you like to say about this story? What did you notice about it? What stands out for you? Do you have any questions?

Deepening students' understanding of the book

Ask the students to re-tell the story. There may be some disagreement about what actually happens in it. Refer to the book. Ask what students think the story is really about. There are different interpretations of this story. Draw out as many as possible. For this unit, though, we want to focus students' attention on it as a story of people working together to nourish each other and have fun; in short, building community. Ask the students to write down their first thoughts about what the story is saying about building community. What's the message of the story? After the students have had a chance to put their thoughts on paper, discuss the question with the class.

Ask the students to make two columns on a sheet of paper. Have them put the word soldier at the top of one column and villager at the top of the other. Ask them to list things the soldiers could have done to get food (for example, worked for it, stolen it, begged, promised to pay later, bartered clothing or boots). List responses the villagers could have made to the soldiers (for example, given food, hidden food, given a little, told the soldiers to work, offered to trade for a sword). Have them share their lists with a classmate. They can pick ideas they like from their partner's list and put it on theirs. Give several volunteers a chance to share their lists with the class and discuss.

At many points in the story, the soldiers and the villagers make choices about what to do. Say that you're going to read the story again and during this reading you want them to pay special attention to the choices people make.[2] Some places to note are on p. 2, when one soldier says that there's no harm in asking, recalling the old phrase, "If you don't ask, you don't get." At the same time, the villagers "feared strangers." Why do we think they feared them? Would they be more afraid of soldiers than of regular strangers? On p. 12, the soldiers respond to the lack of hospitality by saying they will teach the villagers to make stone soup. They are armed. Could they have come back at night and stolen the food, or even forced it from the villagers at sword point? Why didn't they choose to do that?

Suggest that the students imagine themselves as one of the characters in the story. Ask them to pick a character, close their eyes, and try to see that character in their mind. Take a few breaths. Would they have made the same choice or choices that their character does? Why? Why not?

---

[2] Before you do the second reading of the book, you may want to choose a question or two for the students to follow and to answer informally in writing before discussion. Or you might ask them to jot down a few thoughts on a question you ask after the reading. This informal writing often encourages more students to speak during the discussion and allows all children to articulate their thoughts, not just those who are comfortable speaking in groups.

Connecting the book to students' lives[3]

Discussion: Ask the students to think about ritual meals in their families, such as Thanksgiving, birthdays, religious holidays. Do they invite guests to these meals? Does your school have community rituals, such as a school potluck dinner, a school fair, a concert or performance for the parents? How are these events like stone soup?

Have the students tell their read-aloud partners about a time in their lives when they worked with others to achieve a goal or saw others working together (singing in a choir or chorus, a bake sale, a fair, a block party). Ask the partners to share, with permission, what they have heard.

Writing: Ask the students to make a chart of the people in their families. Under each name, write some of the good qualities that each person brings to the family. Students should be sure to include themselves.

Draw and write about a game you are playing in which everyone must contribute an idea or an object. What happens?

Write about a food in your house that is special to you or that you try to keep for yourself but that you would contribute to the soup or to the feast.

ROLE-PLAY

Divide the students into groups of four and ask each group to chose a scene from the story and act it out. If the skits go well and interest is high, the groups might present their skits to the class.

Applied Learning

Lesson 1

Objectives

Students will
- practice paying close attention to others and their classroom environment;
- identify similarities and differences between the community portrayed in *Stone Soup* and the classroom;
- brainstorm qualities of an ideal classroom community.

---

[3] Most of the ideas in this section in all the units are suited to drawing and writing activities. Young children may draw and then dictate or write a caption or story. At all ages, the writing may be informal, as in a reading-response journal or just a regular paper or notebook or, if a seed idea seems appropriate, students may work more on a piece. Writing is a powerful way for each child to think about ideas, and we encourage its use.

Unit 1: Building Community   Grade 3

Materials Needed
- Hugg-a-Planet
- agenda on chart paper or the chalkboard
- chart paper to record students ideas of their ideal classroom community
- collage materials or soup ingredients

Gathering: Name Game

Have the students stand in a circle. Toss a Hugg-A-Planet or other soft object to a child. When the child catches it, the child calls out her or his full name and then everyone yells, "Yes!" The child then throws the object to someone else. Encourage students to pay close attention to who has the Hugg-A-Planet. How do you know when that person is ready to throw it? What can that person look for to know whether someone else is ready to receive it?

Check agenda

Go over the objectives and agenda.

Vision of classroom community

Ask, how is our classroom like the community portrayed in *Stone Soup*? How is it different? The soldiers don't have food to contribute to the soup, but they contribute something. What do they contribute?

Ask the students to brainstorm qualities of their ideal classroom community. The classroom is also a community where people share their resources and cooperate to create something together that we can't create separately.

Do either (or both) of the classroom community-building activities described below:

Have the students **make collages** with various materials (cotton, balloons, yarn, feathers, rubber bands, pipe cleaners, glue, various colors of construction paper). The only requirement is that there be a stone in the middle of it. Students should work together in groups to create the collage and then present the collage to the class. Discuss: How was it to work with a group to make the collage? What does the stone represent? As we build community in our classroom, who, like the soldiers in the story, will provide vision and leadership? What can each of us contribute? Brainstorm a list.

OR Have the group **make stone soup**. Ask everyone to bring something from home. If you do not have cooking facilities in the classroom, make it something like stone fruit soup or stone salad, where everyone brings in something that can be eaten cold. If you have access to a stove or hot plate, ask everyone to bring in one item. Even one carrot is fine. You provide a clean stone. Don't forget the salt and pepper. After this experience, discuss: how was it to make and eat stone soup? As we build community in the classroom, what can each of us contribute? Brainstorm a list.

Grade 3 — Stone Soup

Evaluation

What was most fun for you about today's lesson? Ask for a couple of volunteers to share their thoughts with the group.

Closing: High Five

High five: You and the children are standing in a circle. Give the child to your right the "high five." That child gives high five to the next child, and so it goes, all around the circle.

Lesson 2

Objectives

Students will
- identify behaviors that make for poor listening;
- identify behaviors that make for good listening;
- develop a chart of guidelines for good listening;
- express their opinions and see that differences of opinion are okay.

Materials Needed

- agenda on chart paper or the chalkboard
- chart paper for writing "Guidelines for Good Listening"
- signs for the "Think Differently" exercise ("Strongly Agree," "Strongly Disagree," "Not sure")

Gathering: Cooper Says*

Introduce the game "Cooper Says." ("Cooper" comes from cooperation.) The game is like Simon Says, except that when children make mistakes, they don't have to sit down and leave the game. After the game, ask how they liked Cooper Says. How do they feel about it compared with Simon Says? Why?

* From *The Friendly Classroom for a Small Planet* by Priscilla Prutzman, et al. New Society Publishers, Gabriola Island, BC, Canada. Copyright © 1988 Children's Creative Response to Conflict, PO Box 271, Nyack, NY 10960. T: (845) 353-1796 / F: (845) 358-4924. Used by permission.

Check agenda

Go over the objectives and the agenda.

Good and poor listening

One of the things that helps people cooperate is being able to listen to each other. Ask for a volunteer from the class to come up front and tell you something. While the person is talking, model poor listening (looking away, fidgeting with clothes or hair, doing something else). Ask how the person felt while you were doing this. Ask the class what the class saw. Now have the person tell you the same information, but model good listening (attention focused on speaker, positive body language, no interrupting). Ask students to pair up with each other and practice good listening for about 30 seconds each. Make a good listening checklist to post on the wall.

Think differently

The villagers were not respectful of the soldiers when they first arrived. In our classroom we want to respect each other's needs and opinions. Ask, what is an opinion? It's a strong belief that people have, sometimes based on fact and sometimes not.

Designate one corner of the room for "strongly agree," the opposite corner for "strongly disagree," and the middle for "not sure." Make signs if necessary. Tell the children you'll say a statement. Ask the students to think for a few moments in silence about their opinion of the statement and then to go to the appropriate place according to whether they agree with the statement, disagree, or aren't sure. Try to think of statements on which children will have a range of opinions. Once the children have taken their places, ask for volunteers from each location to explain their opinion. Encourage some dialogue among children with differing opinions. If children change their minds in the course of the discussion, they can change places. Here are some suggested statements:

- Children shouldn't be required to do homework.
- Children shouldn't be required to attend school.
- Children should be limited to one hour of TV a day.
- Children should wear uniforms in school.
- Children should be allowed to chew gum and eat candy in class.

Evaluation

What's one thing you'll do differently as a result of today's lesson? Ask for several volunteers to share their thoughts with the group.

Closing: Pass the Sound*

Begin by making a sound. "Pass" the sound to a student. Ask the student to imitate the sound you are making and then change it into another sound. S/he passes it to another person who repeats the new sound and changes it again. Continue around the group, encouraging each person to listen closely and observe how the person before them is making the sound.

* From *The Friendly Classroom for a Small Planet* by Priscilla Prutzman, et al. New Society Publishers, Gabriola Island, BC, Canada. Copyright © 1988 Children's Creative Response to Conflict, PO Box 271, Nyack, NY 10960. T: (845) 353-1796 / F: (845) 358-4924. Used by permission.

Lesson 3

Objectives

Students will
- practice observation skills
- define "put-up" and "put-down"
- identify the feelings that put-downs and put-ups tend to set off, as well as the physical signs of those feelings
- identify people in their lives whom they appreciate

Materials Needed

- agenda on chart paper or the chalkboard
- two hearts made from construction paper (pattern on page 15) and tape to fasten them to your chest
- markers of assorted colors

Gathering: Mirroring

Have students face a partner; decide who will be A and who will be B. A begins by moving in place in any way that feels comfortable. B must observe closely and "mirror" A's movements. After a minute or two, have the students pause and reverse roles – B chooses the movements and A must mirror them.

What did you have to do to "mirror" your partner well?

Check agenda

Go over the objectives and the agenda.

Put-ups and put-downs

Explain that a put-down is a negative comment about a person. Elicit examples of put-downs from the story or from life (but don't write them down so as not to reinforce them). Ask the children what they think a put-up is. Elicit examples of put-ups. Make a chart of put-ups. Explain that in our classroom, put-downs are not allowed. Put-ups are welcome. When you and the students hear people using put-ups, you can acknowledge them and add them to the chart.

Have a Heart

Make two hearts from construction paper. Explain that our feelings and our classroom community are greatly affected by how we talk to each other. This exercise illustrates the effects of put-downs.

Tape one of the hearts to your chest. Tell the children a story like the one below, tailored to their age and experience. Each time the child in the story experiences a put-down, rip off a piece of the heart and let it fall to the floor. By the end of the story, the heart will be in pieces. Discuss: How is _____ feeling? Ask: If you could see _____ right now, what do you think she might look like? Encourage discussion of facial expression, posture, how she might be moving, and other clues that might help you know what she is feeling. Students could also pantomime what they think her face and posture might look like. Have you ever had a day like this?

Now tape the second heart to your chest and retell the story with the children supplying put-ups instead of put-downs. When the child receives put-ups, color in the heart with crayons or markers of various colors. Discuss: How is _____ feeling now? Again, ask would be the clues – facial expression, posture, movements – that would let you know how she feels? Allow students to pantomime these. What does this exercise suggest for our classroom?

Story for the Have a Heart Exercise

Jane* had not slept well, and when her father called, she didn't get up. A few minutes later, her father shouted, "Get up, lazybones!" When Jane went into the kitchen for breakfast, her brother was just pouring the last of the cereal into his bowl. "That's what you get for oversleeping," he teased. Jane dressed in a new combination she thought looked cool, but when her sister saw her, she laughed. "That looks stupid," she said. Jane changed clothes, grabbed her book bag, and ran out the door to school. She decided to take a short cut. "Hey, what are you doing around this block?" some boy called to her. "We don't like your type around here." "You're late!" the teacher said when she came into her classroom. He wrote her name on the board. Later, the teacher asked her to read aloud. When she said one of the words wrong, some of the kids laughed. At lunch, when she went to sit down with some girls, they said, "No room here. You'll have to sit over there." On the way home from school, Jane was running along and tripped over a crack in the pavement. She want sprawling down on the street and ripped a hole in her pants. When her mother saw Jane, she saw the hole before she saw the rest of her. "You ruined your pants," she said. "I can't keep you in decent clothes!"

* Substitute a name for Jane that is not the name of anyone in your class.

Evaluation

What's one thing you'll do differently as a result of the lesson today?

Closing: Someone I Appreciate

Each of us has people in our lives that we appreciate. Who is one of those people for you? Give the students a minute or two to talk in pairs and then ask several volunteers to tell the group.

Additional Activities

Hillel the Wise

Tell or read or have the children read the story *Hillel the Wise* (page 16) and explain that people all over the world in various countries and cultures share a similar belief. How does this rule apply to the village in the story and how might it apply in our classroom? There are many places in the world where it is the custom to give the best of everything to the guests even if they are strangers. Being respectful of each other and each other's talents is a key theme. We respect what each person brings to the table. Would this be a good rule for our classroom? Why? Why not?

Make time for silence

During this time the lights are off. No writing, drawing, reading, no gadgets. Just sitting. Encourage students to put their hands on their knees. Students can close their eyes if they want. You can tell them that they can let their minds use the silence as they wish. Or you can suggest ways they might use the silence. For example,

- Practice abdominal breathing (introduced in Unit 2)
- Simply pay attention to your breathing
- Pay attention to sounds you hear in your mind, take yourself to a peaceful place
- Recall a time you had fun
- Recall something you like to do

After the time of silence, ask for a couple of volunteers to share where their minds went during the time. Make time for silence every day, preferably at the same time, such as after lunch or recess or the first and last actions of the day.

By giving students the opportunity to experience time for silence on a daily basis, you'll be instilling a habit that will serve them well for the rest of their lives.

Consider having your students keep a 4Rs journal

Writing (drawing for younger students) is an excellent way to reinforce and consolidate learning. A journal enables students to put all of their Book Talk writing in one place. You can also give them a few minutes after each 4Rs lesson to jot down a few thoughts about what they're taking away or how they're planning to use what they've just learned. If a student tries a new skill, s/he might want to write about what happened. Did it bring a positive result? If a student is stuck in a conflict with someone, s/he might want to do some writing to sort it out and imagine some solutions. You can give them standard journals and encourage them to decorate them.

By having students keep journals, you will be introducing them to a habit or practice that can serve them well the rest of their lives.

Related Books

The Bat Boy and His Violin by Gavin Curtis, illustrated by E.B. Lewis

A Chair for My Mother by Vera Williams

Chicken Sunday by Patricia Polacco

The Dancing Man by Ruth Lercher Bornstein

Grandpa's Soup by Eiko Kadono, illustrated by Satomi Ichikawa

Horton Hears a Who by Dr. Seuss

Grade 3 — Stone Soup

Handout 1 • Unit 1

Pattern for Have a Heart

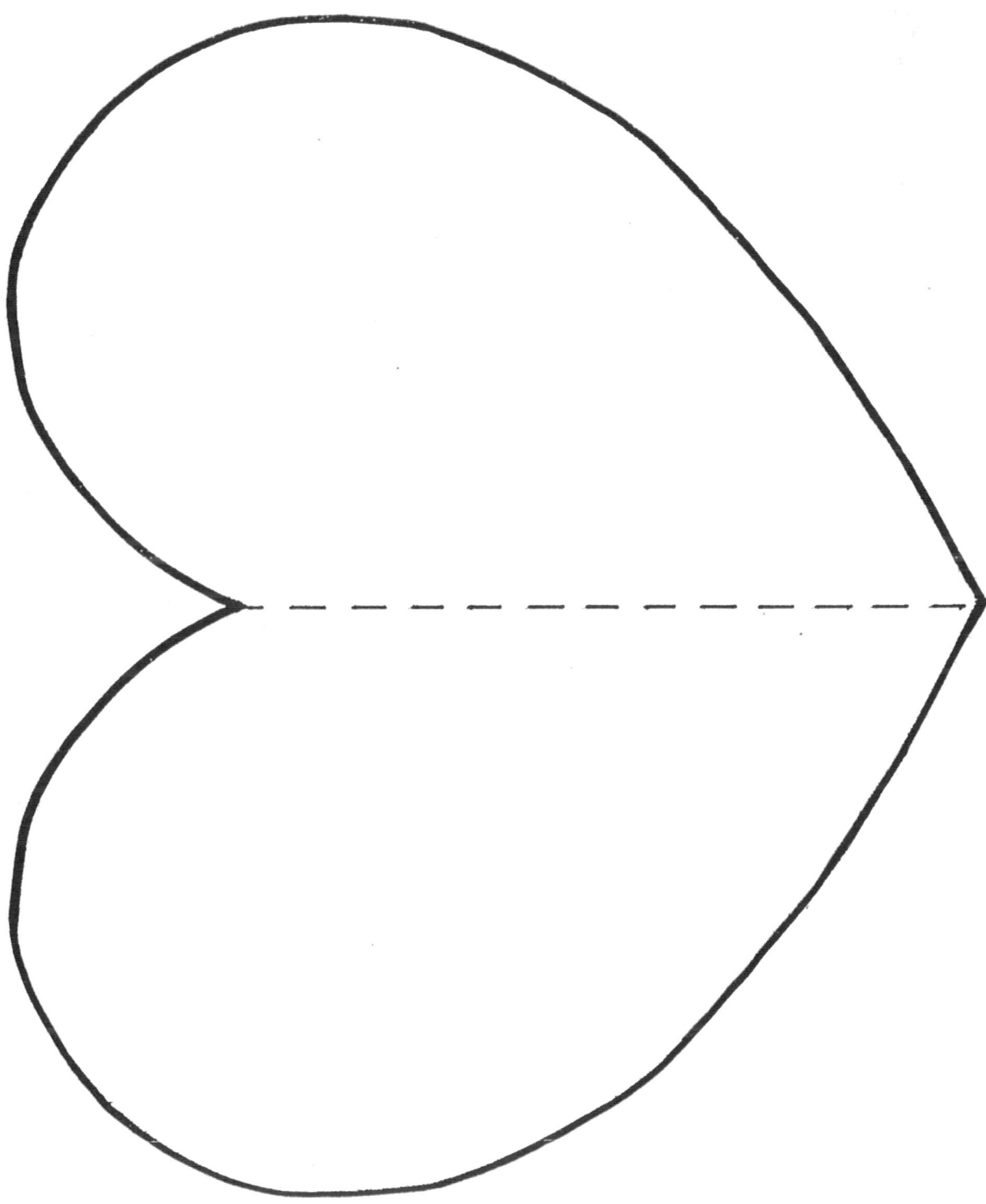

The 4Rs © Morningside Center for Teaching Social Responsibility

Handout 2 • Unit 1

Hillel the Wise

There once was a very wise and learned teacher named Hillel. Now Rabbi Hillel was not only a wise teacher, he was a good and patient teacher. His reputation had spread as far as King Herod's palace. There was a young man in Herod's palace who did not like to study, who did not want to learn. But he did like to make fun of others, and he did like to gamble. So one day he made a bet with his friends that he could show that Rabbi Hillel was not as wise and patient as he was supposed to be. He wagered 400 zuzim that he could make Hillel angry.

For three days he asked Hillel annoying questions, and each time, the rabbi answered patiently and with great wisdom. The young man was afraid he would lose the bet and have to pay 400 zuzim. He stayed up all night thinking of a way to make Hillel angry. The next day, he burst into the study house and stood in front of Hillel. He hopped up and down, saying, "Rabbi, Rabbi, can you teach me the whole of Torah while I stand on one foot?" All the other students were amazed. They spent years studying Torah, the holy book.

Hillel stayed calm. He looked at the young man and said, "That which is hateful unto you, do not do it to your neighbor. That is the whole of Torah. The rest is commentary. Now go and learn."

Many religious traditions have a similar teaching. Christianity uses a "golden rule" similar to Rabbi Hillel's: "Do unto others as you would have them do unto you." Muslims have a teaching in the holy book the Koran that says, "Repel the evil with what is better, and you will see that the worst of enemies can become the best of friends."

Adapted from *While Standing on One Foot, Puzzle Stories and Wisdom Tales from the Jewish Tradition*, by Nina Jaffe and Steve Zeitlin. Henry Holt and Company, Inc., 1993.

3

Unit 2 Theme

Understanding & Managing Feelings

Unit 2 Book Selection

JoJo's Flying Side Kick by Brian Pinkney
Aladdin Paperbacks, Simon & Schuster, 1997

Activities

- Feelings Web
- Mashed Potatoes
- Mirroring
- Stories about Feelings
- Feelings Barometer
- Exploring what happens when we have a strong feeling
- Triggers for fear, nervousness, or anger
- Ways we deal with fear, nervousness, and anger
- Self-talk
- Abdominal ("belly") breathing
- Plan 1-2-3

Introduction

We all have feelings; like conflict, feelings are part of life. But feelings don't need to control our lives or dictate our actions. When feelings come up, we can choose whether to act on them or not and, if so, how. This is one of the most important principles in creating community and in dealing well with conflict.

Understanding that they have feelings and naming them is not always easy for children. Often adults will tell a child, "Be quiet, that didn't hurt," or "That's not something to be upset about," or "Of course you love your baby brother," when the child is feeling something completely different. Children need to acknowledge their feelings and learn to handle them. They need to know that others also have feelings that are expressed in tone of voice, facial expression, and body language. They need to be able to think ahead to the consequences of acting on feelings, to be able to try to predict whether a proposed action will have the intended result.

Much of our energy in the classroom and life in general goes toward negative feelings. We need to celebrate positive feelings and their impact on the community.

Literature offers many opportunities to talk about feelings, as we analyze the actions of characters and the feelings evoked in us, the readers.

In any discussion of conflict and of feelings, anger always comes up and therefore deserves special attention. The American Heritage Dictionary defines anger as a feeling of extreme displeasure, hostility, indignation, or exasperation toward someone or something. Behind anger may lie feelings of fear and hurt. Everyone has anger triggers, but the triggers are different for different people. It is particularly useful for us to become aware of what triggers our anger and that of others so that we can manage the anger rather than letting it control us. Anger is useful in letting us know that needs are not being met. But when anger goes up, thinking tends to go down. We can learn strategies for cooling down so that we can express our anger in a constructive way that respects the other person and is most likely to lead to a positive result.

How to Calm Down When You're Angry

- Leave the situation for a while, saying that you'll be back when you can think more clearly
- Count to ten
- Take deep breaths, focusing your eyes on something pleasant near you
- Talk to yourself: "I can handle this," "I'm not going to let this person make me do something stupid."

Strategies for reducing anger include recognizing that you're angry (by recognizing the anger cues); centering (taking deep breaths, counting to ten); focusing attention on something pleasant (thinking pleasant thoughts, visualizing a favorite place, etc.); and talking to yourself in positive ways ("I can handle this" or "We can work it out").

Once we have calmed down, we can decide what action, if any, to take. It's possible that the situation really just requires a calming down period. If, however, the situation requires action, that action can be taken in an assertive, not aggressive, way, so that it does not escalate the situation.

Anger can be used constructively to change situations. We need to hold fast to and channel what could be called "righteous anger," the indignation at actions and conditions in the world that are unfair. It is this anger that has fueled the work of many well-known religious leaders, visionaries, and social activists.

In this unit

	Ideas	Skills
Literacy	<ul><li>Comparisons</li><li>Hyperbole</li><li>Subplot</li></ul>	<ul><li>Vocabulary in context</li><li>Empathizing</li></ul>
Social and Emotional Learning	<ul><li>All human beings experience a wide range of feelings.</li><li>Identifying and naming our feelings gives us more control over them.</li><li>When feelings arise, we have choices about how to respond.</li><li>When we experience strong feelings, we don't always think clearly.</li><li>We can learn ways to cool down so that we can think more clearly about the smartest thing to do.</li></ul>	<ul><li>Naming feelings</li><li>Reading feelings</li><li>Identifying our anger triggers</li><li>Strategies for cooling down so that we can think more clearly</li><li>Self Talk</li><li>Abdominal breathing</li><li>Plan 1-2-3</li></ul>

JoJo's Flying Side Kick, written and illustrated by Brian Pinkney. Aladdin Paperbacks, Simon & Schuster, 1995.

SUMMARY

JoJo is practicing her flying side kick at the Tae Kwon Do center. Her teacher tells her that she is doing so well that the next day she will take a test to move from white belt to yellow belt status. She is very nervous at the thought. As she walks home with her grandfather, we learn that she is also nervous about the large tree in her front yard, which to her looks like a "creepy bandit." Her grandfather asks if she's worried about the test. "'I'm freakin'out,' she replies." Her grandfather responds by telling her that when he used to box he would do "'a little shuffle to keep the jitters away.'" JoJo is polite and even practices some moves, but she doesn't see the relevance to her situation. Her friend P.J. walks by and tells her he doesn't think she's strong enough to break the wood. Instead of responding defensively, JoJo asks why. He tells her that she needs to put more power into her voice, which means that the sound has to come "'from deep down in your stomach.'" She shrugs off this advice, too, all the time being wary of the tree. When P.J. and his dog leave, she imagines the tree lunging at her and runs in fear to her house. Inside, her mother, too, has advice for the upcoming exam: "'Visualize. . . . Picture yourself doing the perfect flying side kick.'" JoJo tries, but sees only shadows in her head. She can't sleep, worrying both about the test and the tree/bandit, which in her dream tries to climb into her room. The next day, "butterflies fluttered in her stomach." She tries her grandfather's shuffle, but when she looks at the board she must break, she freezes. However, she has synthesized the advice she has received and uses it to fight her personal demon and pass the test. She visualizes the tree bandit and from deep in her stomach screams "'Keeyyaahhh!'" and splits the board. Her proud mother and grandfather applaud as she receives the yellow belt. On the way home, she insists on swinging on the swing hanging from the tree. When her grandfather says he thought she didn't like that swing, she "just smiled, threw back her head, and kicked up to the sky."

COMMENT

This book speaks to the very real fears children have in everyday life as well as in test situations. The adults are supportive and offer good advice. Her friend P.J. is less supportive, but his bluntness is helpful. She chooses to learn from his advice rather than get into a conflict with him over his opinion of her abilities. She learns that she must face her fears herself and that she can use the support of others to find her own way in the world. She does not have to let her fear limit her life. In fact, once she conquers fear in one area, she finds she has conquered it in another. We can ask what strategies we can use when we have a test of whatever sort or when we are afraid of something or someone.

Book Talk

READ-ALOUD

Previewing the book

Show the complete cover of the book. What do the students notice about the cover? What do they think the book is about? What does the typeface remind them of? Why would the author choose this typeface? Have they read other books by this author? Did the other books use the same type of drawings? Read the note from the author and the author information at the front and back inside covers. Do any of the students in the room do Tae Kwon Do? Do any of them study another martial art?

Reading and responding to the book

Read the book slowly, giving the students time to look at the pictures. The process by which the pictures were made is very painstaking and creates intensely vibrant colors. As you look closely, you see the many layers of paint that have been scratched to create an overall effect. Explain that the scenes in the Tae Kwon Do center take place in front of a mirror. As in a dance studio, the students need to see their work reflected.

After you have finished reading the story, ask the children, what would you like to say about this story? Do you have any questions?

Deepening students' understanding of the book

Ask the students to recall what happened in the story. Students may focus on JoJo's imagination or on her flying side kick.[1] Get as many ideas as possible from the group. For this unit, we are looking at the idea of overcoming fear by using our inner resources and the support of those around us.

In the second reading, students should pay special attention to the advice JoJo gets from her family and friend as well as on JoJo's feelings. After the reading, ask students to recall the advice JoJo receives. Do they agree with the advice? In general, when adults give advice, do the students find it helpful?

During the second reading, students can also pay close attention to the language.

---

[1] Students may have questions about Tae Kwon Do. There are many different styles of Tae Kwon Do. The author has studied Tae Kwon Do for nine years. However, the situation he describes may not correspond to the experience of students in the class who are familiar with Tae Kwon Do. That is, in some centers the test would not be given to an individual but to a group, with extensive preparation. It would include much, much more than a flying side kick, which in any case would not be a qualification for a yellow belt but for a more advanced belt. It is possible that the author has used poetic license in describing some of the processes involved in moving from one belt color to the next. We don't know whether in a small town such as JoJo's things are done differently or whether he changed facts to move the plot forward. Fiction writers often change facts to make the story go better.

The author uses a technique called personification. That is, when something that is not alive is described as if it were. In this case, the tree becomes a creepy bandit. Ask students to write down some other personification they have heard or read. (The rock stood guard at the entrance to the cave. The light danced on the water.)

The author also uses figures of speech (butterflies in the stomach) to describe an emotion. Can students list some other figures of speech that describe feelings (tied up in knots, cat got your tongue, scared silly)? You may want to explain the difference between a figure of speech and a simile (happy as a clam, quiet as a mouse, happy as a pig in mud, clumsy as a bull in a china shop).

Below are some suggested stopping points for the second reading:

p. 4 "Then she began to worry." What are the things she may be worrying about?

p. 6 "It looked like a creepy bandit." If you were scared of it, what would it look like to you? If you weren't scared of it, what would it look like?

p. 9 "'. . . butterflies fluttered in my stomach before a very big boxing match.'" This is a metaphor for what feeling(s)?

p. 11 " 'I don't think you're strong enough to break a piece of wood tomorrow,' P.J. said." How do you think this makes JoJo feel? What could she have said?

p. 13 "JoJo froze." What are some words for what she is feeling now?

p. 15 "Visualize." What do you think this means?

p. 21 ". . .she froze." Do you think this is the same kind of freezing as before? What do you think she is feeling?

p. 22 "JoJo just smiled, threw back her head, and kicked up to the sky." How is Jo Jo feeling now? Why is she able to swing on the swing now?

Connecting the book to students' lives

Pairs and then a go round: JoJo is nervous about the test she will be taking for her yellow belt. She tells her grandfather, "I'm freakin' out!" All of us have times in our lives when we're nervous about something. Sometimes we even feel we're freakin' out.

Ask the students to pair up and tell their partners about a time when they were nervous (or even freakin' out) about something. What were they nervous about? Did people try to help them by giving advice? What did they do? How did it turn out? Model the activity by telling the students a brief story of a time you faced a challenge you were nervous about.

After the students have talked in pairs for a few minutes, send the talking piece around, inviting students to tell their stories.

Writing: Have the students write up the story they told in go round. Encourage them to draw a picture to illustrate their story.

Ask students to write stories about a time they or someone else was fearful.

ROLE-PLAY

Ask the students to work in pairs and act out the scene between JoJo and P.J. Why do you think P.J. tells her she won't pass? Has anything like this ever happened to you?

Applied Learning

Lesson 1

Objectives

Students will
- play a name game to learn and give "shout-outs" for each other's names
- recall words from the story that name feelings and brainstorm other "feelings words" they know to create a feelings web
- play a game called "Mashed Potatoes"
- play a game called "Mirroring"
- tell stories about times they experienced a particular feeling

Materials

- Agenda on chart paper or the chalkboard
- Poster board or chart paper for making the feelings web
- Hugg-A-Planet or other soft object for the name game
- Talking piece

Gathering: Name Game

Play the name game again, as in Unit 1. Have the students stand in a circle. Toss a Hugg-A-Planet or other soft object to a student. When the student catches it, s/he calls out her or his full name and then everyone yells, "Yes!" S/he then throws the ball to someone else, and so on around the circle till everyone has had a turn. Encourage students to pay close attention to who has the Hugg-A-Planet. How do you know when that person is ready to throw it? What can that person look for to know whether someone else is ready to receive it?

Check agenda

Go over the objectives and the agenda.

Feelings Web

Tell the students that you need their help to create a "feelings web." Write the word "feelings" in the middle of a piece of chart paper and draw a circle around it. Begin the web by asking the students to recall feelings experienced by the characters in the story. Record their responses. When they run out of ideas, read passages of the story in which other feelings are named or expressed and chart those words. Then see how many other feelings words your group can generate in a few minutes. Your web might start out looking something like this.

Tell the students that you'll keep the web and post it for each session. As feelings words come up in discussions, songs, poems, and stories throughout the school year, add those words to the web to build the students' feelings vocabularies.

Mashed Potatoes

Explain that the class will now play a game called "Mashed Potatoes." A student will choose a feeling word from the web of feelings words and say "mashed potatoes" in a way that expresses the feeling. The class has to guess the feeling. Model the activity by choosing a feelings word and acting out "mashed potatoes" yourself for the students to guess. Give various students turns as long as interest remains high.

Discuss: It's not only what a person says but how s/he says it that tells us what s/he's feeling.

For a variation on this activity, write feeling words on 3x5 cards and put them in a basket. Choose a student to come up front, close eyes, and draw a card from the basket. Taking turns, students act out "mashed potatoes," expressing the feelings on the cards for the class to guess.

Mirroring

Repeat the "mirroring" activity from Unit 1, Lesson 3. Have students face a partner. Decide who will be A and who will be B. This time, A should focus on changing facial expressions to express or emotions from the chart of "feelings words." B must observe closely and "mirror" A's facial expressions and then guess the feeling. . After a minute or two, have the students reverse roles: B chooses a feeling and makes facial expressions that express the feeling and A must mirror them and name the feeling.

Stories about Feelings

Explain that now you're going to ask the students to tell a story about a time they experienced a particular feeling. They can choose a feeling from the Feelings Web Chart or another feeling. Model the activity by telling a story about a feeling you experienced. Describe where you were, what may have triggered the feeling, who else was present (if anyone), whether the feeling led you to do something, and, if so, what you did and how it turned out. Now send the talking piece around for students to share.

Reflection/Feedback and Closing

Send the talking piece around for students to say one word that expresses how they're feeling right now.

Lesson 2

Objectives

Students will
- reflect on how they're feeling, give their feeling a number, and put an x in the appropriate place on the feelings barometer
- recall a recent time when they experienced a strong feeling—fear, nervousness, or anger
- identify what went on in their mind and body when they felt the strong feeling

Materials

- Hugg-A-Planet
- Agenda on chart paper or the chalkboard
- Web of feelings words from Unit 2, Lesson 1 (in case additional feelings words come up to add to the web)
- Copies of the lyrics to "If You're Happy and You Know It" for you and the students, if necessary (see handout)
- A "feelings barometer" (a piece of chart paper with a horizontal line on top of which are numbers from -5 to +5)
- Chart paper with three columns with these headings: "fear," " nervousness," "anger"
- Talking piece

Gathering: "If you're happy and you know it"

You and your students are probably familiar with this song. If not, see the handout for the words and ask a colleague in your school or go on YouTube for the tune. This song is fun to use anytime as a gathering or a closing for a 4Rs lesson, or anytime your class needs a pick-me-up.

Unit 2: Feelings Grade 3

Check agenda

Go over the objectives and the agenda.

Feelings Barometer

Explain that a barometer is an instrument that can help predict the weather by measuring air pressure in the atmosphere. Show them the feelings barometer. Explain that the feelings barometer can help us measure the emotional weather in the classroom.

Explain that in a minute you'll be asking students to come up and put an x under the number that best represents their overall feeling today. A –5 would be the worst way a student could be feeling. A +5 would be the best way a student could be feeling. Ask the students for reasons that might cause them to put an x under -5, or -2, or +3, and or +5.

Model the activity by putting an x under the number that represents how you're feeling and explain briefly why you're putting your x there. Ask whether there are any questions. Once the students understand how the feelings barometer works, have them come up in groups of three or four for each to put an x under the number that best represents how they're feeling right now. When all students are done, the feelings barometer might look something like this.

-5	-4	-3	-2	-1	0	+1	+2	+3	+4	+5
x		x	x	x	x		x	x		x
		x	x	x	x		x	x		
			x		x		x	x		

Without calling attention to any one student's x, ask for any general observations students want to make about the feelings barometer. Where do most of our feelings lie today? How does the group as a whole seem to be feeling? Is something going on in school that might explain the group's overall feeling—for example, a test or a basketball game with another school that everyone is looking forward to?

You can use the feelings barometer from time to time to gauge the emotional state of your group. You may want to keep and date the charts for comparison purposes.

Exploring what happens when we have a strong feeling

In the story, JoJo's grandfather asks if she's worried about the test. She replies, "I'm freakin' out!" What does she mean? How is she feeling? Call on a couple of volunteers to explain. Elicit that JoJo means she's super scared or nervous.

Ask the students if they've ever freaked out. If so, what did they freak out about? What were they scared or nervous about? Call on a couple of volunteers to describe the situations.

Now ask the students to think of times when they were angry. Call on a couple of volunteers to give examples.

Explain that today in 4Rs you're going to help the students become aware of the thoughts, feelings, and bodily sensations people tend to experience when they're scared or angry.

Ask the students to think of a time recently when they were scared or nervous about something. Or, if they prefer, they can think about at time recently when they were angry. Give them a minute or so to think of a time. Tell them to give a "thumbs up" when they have a situation in mind. Once most of the students have thought of something, ask for one or two volunteers to share their situations briefly with the group. Encourage any students who are having difficulty to think of a time and give them another minute to do so.

Now tell the class that you want each of them to recall their situation as fully as they can. As they sit silently in their seats, ask them the questions below, pausing after each question to give time for them to recall the details. You don't want them to answer the questions out loud, but to create a full picture of the situation in their mind's eye.

- Where were you?
- Who were you with (if anybody)?
- What were you doing?
- What was the place like?
- What time of day was it?
- What were the people wearing?
- What were they saying?
- What were you saying and doing?
- What were you feeling? Anger? Fear? Nervousness? A mixture of both? Some other feeling?
- Can you recall what was going on in your body — your heart, your lungs, your stomach, your arms, your legs, your face?
- Can you recall what was going on in your mind? What were you thinking? What were you saying to yourself?

Suggest, "Before we begin, let's all take a deep breath together." Lead them in taking a deep breath. Now ask them to pair up to share their story with a partner.

At the end of the pair-share, invite the class to take another deep breath together, as if they are taking in the stories they have heard.

Send the talking piece around for students to share their stories with the whole group. Prompt students with the following questions:

- What feeling were you having?
- What was going on in your body?

- What were you thinking?
- What pictures came into your mind?

As students share, record the students' feelings, thoughts, pictures, and bodily sensations on a T-chart, differentiating among anger, fear and nervousness, as follows:

Anger	Fear	Nervousness
• face getting warm • heart beating fast • "I feel like punching that guy • "It's not fair."	• heart pounding • cold sweat • "I'm outta here!"	• butterflies in my stomach • "I'm freakin' out!" • mouth and throat dry • jitters

After the go round, ask students to take a look at the chart. What do they want to say about the chart? Maybe someone will say that some of the bodily sensations for anger are similar those for fear and others are different. Share any comments you want to make about the chart.

Point out to the students that these responses are normal. Anger, fear, and nervousness are part of life. We all experience them at one time or another. When we get angry, scared, or nervous, our bodies mobilize for action, and our thoughts support the process. But sometimes our minds and bodies overreact. We don't necessarily have to act on our feelings. In fact, in some cases, it's best to calm down if we can so that we can think more clearly about what to do.

Reflection/Feedback and Closing

Ask students to talk in pairs to share something they might do today to move their overall mood to a higher number on the feelings barometer. Call on a couple of students to share what they plan to do.

Lesson 3

Objectives

Students will
- identify their triggers for fear, nervousness, and anger
- share ways they deal with feelings of fear, nervousness, and anger

Materials

- Chart paper with the heading "Triggers" and, underneath the heading, columns for fear, nervousness, and anger (see chart below)
- Chart paper with the heading, "Strategies for Times When We're Freakin' Out"

- Lyrics to "I Whistle a Happy Tune" for the Closing (see handout)
- Talking piece

Gathering: Squeeze-Relax

To help students relax as you begin today's lesson, ask them to tighten or squeeze the muscles in their feet, hold for three to five seconds, and then relax. Continue with legs, back, stomach, chest, hands, arms, shoulder, neck and face. Finish by asking students to squeeze all their muscles at the same time, hold for three to five seconds, and relax. Ask a few volunteers to describe what this was like for them.

Check agenda

Go over the objectives and the agenda

Triggers for Fear, Nervousness, and Anger

Explain that a "fear trigger" is something that makes us afraid. A "nervousness trigger" is something that makes us nervous. An "anger trigger" is something that makes us angry. In the story, what was a nervousness trigger for JoJo? What was a fear trigger for JoJo? Call on a couple of students to recall JoJo's triggers.

Ask, If a "fear trigger" is something we find scary, what would an "anger trigger" be? Elicit that it's something that makes us angry. Call on a couple of students to give examples of things that make them angry.

Ask the students to pair up. "In a minute I want you to talk with your partner about your triggers—your fear, nervousness, and anger triggers. In other words, you'll think of things that bring up feelings of fear, nervousness, and anger. First, though, let's all take a deep breath together." Model breathing deeply and ask students to join you in doing so.

Now ask the students to talk with their partners about something that scares them—things like the tree in the story that reminded JoJo of a "creepy bandit." After a couple of minutes, call on students to share their fear triggers. Record their responses as in the chart below.

Repeat the activity with nervousness and again with anger. Your chart might start off looking something like this.

Fear Triggers	Nervousness Triggers	Anger Triggers
<ul><li>A teacher yelling at me</li><li>A bully</li><li>Thunder and lightning</li></ul>	<ul><li>Tests in school</li><li>When the teacher calls on me</li><li>The first day of school</li></ul>	<ul><li>When I get blamed for something I didn't do</li><li>When my sister is late to pick me up</li><li>When someone jumps in front of me in line</li></ul>

When students are done sharing, invite the class to take a slow, deep breath together. Again, model taking a deep breath and then invite the class to join you.

Ask them to look at the chart of their responses. Pick one or more of the columns and read the triggers going down the list. After reading each trigger, ask students who have that trigger to raise their hands.

Discuss: Why can it be helpful for us to be aware of our triggers?

Dealing with fear, nervousness, and anger

Ask students to recall the ways JoJo dealt with her fears and the upcoming test. (She visualized the tree bandit and followed P.J.'s advice to scream *Keeyyaahhh!* from keep down inside as she was making her kick. We can also assume that she prepared for her test by working hard to strengthen her body and practice her kicks.)

Ask the students, What do you do when you're freakin' out about something? Give an example from your own life of a situation that made you nervous and what you did to deal with the situation. Call on a couple of students to give examples of things they do when they're freakin' out.

Now ask all of the students to talk in pairs about a time they were freakin' out about something and what they did, if anything, to deal with their fear and the situation.

After students have talked in pairs, send the talking piece around for students to share a time when they were freakin' out and what they did to deal with the feeling. As they share, chart their responses under the heading "Ways We Deal with Things That Freak Us Out."

> **Ways We Deal with Things that Freak Us Out**
> - Cry
> - Ask for help from a parent
> - Talk to a friend
> - Go into my room and shut the door
> - Play a video game
> - Listen to music
> - Count to ten

When all of the students have had the opportunity to share, ask the class to look at the chart.

Discuss: What would they like to say about the chart? Do the ideas listed here give you ideas that may be helpful the next time you're freakin' out?

Share your own observations as well. You may see that many of the students are using the same kinds of strategies. Or perhaps few of them are using any strategies at all. Whatever you see in the chart, point it out to the students and keep any insights in mind for follow up.

Closing

Introduce students to the song "I Whistle a Happy Tune." Use your phone or a computer to find it on YouTube and play it for your students. See handout with the lyrics).

After introducing the song to the students, ask how they feel about whistling a happy turn when they're afraid. Do they think that would work for them?

Once students have learned the words to the song, they can add facial expressions and body postures to act out some of the feelings mentioned in the song ("afraid," "I hold my head erect," "shivering in my shoes," "a careless pose," "happiness," "brave").Does changing your facial expression or posture change how you feel?

Lesson 4

Objectives

Students will
- be introduced to self-talk as a way to cool down when triggered
- be introduced to abdominal ("belly') breathing as a way to cool down and center themselves

Materials

- A balloon for the abdominal breathing activity
- Copies of the "Triggers and Self-Talk" handout for students
- Agenda on chart paper

Gathering: Ballooning*

Ask students what it looks like when a balloon is blown up and then the air is let out. Have them stand and, on the count of three, take in a deep breath and raise their arms as if they were a balloon filling with air. Hold for a second on two, then have them release the air and lower their arms, "deflating" into a small shape. Students may have different ways of doing this. Repeat two more times.

Ask the students how they found the activity. Do they think it would be helpful to do it when they're feeling nervous about something?

* Adapted from *Creative Conflict Resolution* by William Kreidler, p. 120.

Unit 2: Feelings Grade 3

Check agenda

Go over the objectives and the agenda, explaining that today students will learn two strategies for calming themselves down when they're scared, nervous, or angry. When we experience strong feelings, it's hard to think clearly. By calming down when we're scared, nervous, or angry, we can think better about how to deal with the situation.

Self-Talk

Explain that one of the best strategies for calming ourselves down is to talk to ourselves!

For example, when something happens to trigger our anger, we can make ourselves angrier or calmer by what we say to ourselves.

Let's say that an adult yells at you and blames you for something you didn't do, and that triggers your anger. You can react out of anger and curse at the adult or kick a chair or whatever. But you have another choice. You can pause, catch yourself before you react, and silently say something to yourself like "S/he must be having a bad day, but s/he's not going to ruin mine by getting me in trouble."

By doing that, you're on the way to cooling down. It's not okay for the person to blame you unfairly and treat you disrespectfully, but if you can calm yourself down, you have a better chance of making a good choice about the smartest thing for you to do in the situation.

Distribute the "Triggers and Self-Talk" handout. Ask them to choose one of their triggers for fear, anger, or nervousness. They should write it down on the paper—for example, "being blamed for something I didn't do." Then they should think of something they might say to themselves to calm themselves down when they are triggered in that way. They should write that down on the handout as well.

Ask, Would any of you be able to give an example of a trigger and something you might say to yourself to calm yourself down? Call on a couple of students to give examples. If necessary, give an example or two yourself. When you think that the students understand what to do, tell them to get started.

Circulate to help those who are struggling. After about two minutes, send the talking piece around for students to share what they've written.

> NOTE: Here are some typical examples of self-talk: "I won't let you ruin my day." "This is not about me." "I won't take the bait." In self-talk, humor can be useful as well. You might say (to yourself) something absurd, like "Your donkey is wearing a purple polka dot overcoat." Anything that makes you smile in your mind will lower the trigger response and be useful.

In conclusion, point out two crucial things to remember about self-talk:
- You say it in your mind, not out loud.

- Talking to yourself to cool down is a good way to buy time to think about the best way to deal with the situation.

*Abdominal Breathing (Sometimes Called "Belly Breathing")***

Point out that there have been times during this unit that you have asked students to take a deep breath together. Ask, Why do you think we have been taking those deep breaths?

Introduce the idea that deep breathing can help us calm down and cool down when we are feeling strong emotions. This can help us think more clearly when we are scared, nervous, or angry. In this activity, students will practice deep breathing and increase their awareness of its effects.

Ask students to close their eyes and pay attention to their breathing. Are they breathing through their nose or through their mouth? Are their chests and bellies moving as they breathe? Call on several volunteers to share what they noticed.

Ask, Why do we breathe? Why is breathing important?

Point out that most of the time we pay little attention to our breathing; we breathe without even thinking about it. But there are times when it's useful to pay attention to our breathing and breathe in a special way.

One special way of breathing is called abdominal breathing. Ask whether any students know what the abdomen is. Elicit or explain that it's a part of our body—our belly. Abdominal breathing is a special kind of breathing in which our belly expands (moves out) and then contracts (moves in)—and out and in, and out and in.

> NOTE: You can use a balloon to help students understand what goes on when we breathe. Blow the balloon up to half its capacity, let some air out, then blow it back up to half capacity. Explain that we have two lungs in our chests. When we breathe in, our lungs fill part way up with air. When we breathe out, they go down, or contract—like the balloon. When our breathing is shallow, our chest and lungs don't move very much. But if we breathe deeply, the lungs expand a lot. A muscle called the diaphragm, which is underneath the lungs and helps the lungs expand, pushes the organs in our abdomen down and out. So as our lungs expand to full capacity, our chest and belly expand too.

Illustrate by blowing the balloon up to full capacity. Explain that as our lungs fill up with air and grow larger, the belly and the chest move out to make room for them.

Tell the students that you want them to try it. You'll show them how it's done. Put the palm of your hand on your abdomen. Breathe in deeply and slowly while expanding your belly and chest. Then breathe out slowly, contracting your belly. Ask the students what they noticed as you were breathing deeply in and out. Elicit that you breathed slowly and that your hand—and your belly beneath it—moved out as you took air in and in as you breathed air out.

Unit 2: Feelings Grade 3

Explain that you want them to do three cycles, each cycle consisting of one breath in and one breath out. Suggest that when they slowly breathe in (belly expanding), they can silently think, "In…" When they slowly breathe out (belly contracting), they can silently think, "Out…" Tell them to begin and do it with them. When you have done three cycles, ask, How was that for you? Was it easy to breathe in with your belly expanding and out with it contracting? How did it feel? Are there benefits to pausing sometimes to breathe this way? If they think so, what might they be? Elicit that abdominal breathing brings more oxygen into our lungs and helps us be healthy. Deep breathing also helps us relax and cool down. With more oxygen in our brains, we tend to think better.

Acknowledge that since abdominal breathing is a special kind of breathing, it takes practice. The more we do it, the more skilled we'll become.

** Adapted from *Building Emotional Intelligence: Techniques to Cultivate Inner Strength in Children* by Linda Lantieri, pp. 74-76. The book is a great source of ideas for helping children relax their bodies and focus their minds.

Evaluation and Closing

Ask students to complete this sentence: A time/place in my life when I could use abdominal breathing is…

Lesson 5

Objectives

Students will learn and practice Plan 1-2-3 for doing the right thing when their triggered

Materials

- agenda on chart paper or the chalkboard
- chart Plan 1-2-3 (see below)

Gathering: Pausing to Breathe

Turn off the lights n the classroom. Lead the students in doing a couple of cycles of abdominal breathing, as in the previous lesson: hand on belly, belly goes out while airs comes into the lungs, belly comes in while air goes out. Notice whether there are any who need help and make a note to assist them at another time.

Now ask the students to close their eyes and do three cycles of abdominal breathing with their eyes closed. Join them in doing the three cycles.

With the lights still off, ask the students how this was for them. How did they feel doing this? Do they go anywhere in their minds while they were breathing deeply? If so, where? What did they think about? Call on a couple of volunteers to share.

> NOTE: *Pausing to Breathe* is an activity you may want to do at other times in the day—for example, first thing in the morning or when students return from lunch. It will help them calm down and be more focused. You may find it useful, too.

Check agenda

Go over the objectives and the agenda.

Plan 1-2-3

We've shared strategies we use for times when we're afraid, nervous, or angry, and learned about self talk and abdominal breathing. Today we're going to learn about another way to deal with situations in which we're scared or angry. It's called Plan 1-2-3 because it's as easy as 1, 2, 3.

Show them the chart of Plan 1-2-3 (below) and ask a volunteer to read the three steps.

> **1. Stop**
> **2. Breathe**
> **3. Think**

Now say that you'll tell them more about each step of Plan 1-2-3. You want them to remember the three steps and what you say about them. They need to pay attention. After you've explained the three steps to them, you'll ask them to work in pairs to quiz each other on the steps.

Walk them through the steps, referring to the chart, and provide the following explanations:

Step 1 is to STOP yourself when you feel yourself getting upset <u>before you react</u>. Pay attention to your body and your mind. What are you thinking? What is your body saying to you? How are you feeling?

Step 2 is to BREATHE. Here's where abdominal breathing comes in. Take a few moments to breathe deeply—in and out, and in and out, and in and out. This will help you calm down a bit and think more clearly.

Step 3 is to THINK. After pausing and taking a few deep breaths, ask yourself, What is the smartest thing for me to do right now? Maybe the smartest thing is to do nothing. Maybe the smartest thing is to tell the other person how you're feeling in a strong but not mean way. We can be pretty sure that hitting or saying mean things is NOT the smartest thing to do. Think of your choices. Think of the consequences.

Unit 2: Feelings — Grade 3

Tell the students that as our year with The 4Rs goes on, they will be learning that they have choices when they're angry or scared or in conflict. They'll explore the consequences of various actions. That will increase their skill in using Plan 1-2-3.

Now ask students to pair up and quiz each other on the steps. They should ask each other to say the three steps and give an explanation of each.

After students have had a few minutes to work in pairs, cover the chart of Plan 1-2-3 and call on a couple of volunteers to recite the three steps and describe what's involved in each.

Now it's time to practice Plan 1-2-3

Practicing Plan 1-2-3

Ask the students to form two lines facing each other so that each person has a partner. If you have an odd number of students, you'll be someone's partner. Ask the students to shake hands with their partners.

Explain that they will be "thought partners," putting their heads together to think of creative ways to deal with situations that trigger their anger. You are going to describe a situation in which students' anger might be triggered, and take the students through the steps of Plan 1-2-3 to deal with it.

Use situations of your own devising or from the box below. Here are steps you might follow:

- Describe the situation to the students

- Ask them to imagine themselves in this situation—that it is really happening to them. Ask students to give you a thumbs-up when they are picturing themselves in the situation.

- Now it's time for Plan 1-2-3. Ask, What's Step 1? Okay, let's do it. STOP and imagine how you'd be feeling. What would be going through your mind? What would be going on in your body? Call on several volunteers to share.

- What is Step 2? Okay, let's all BREATHE together. Lead them in taking a couple of deep breaths.

- What's Step 3? Okay, take a couple of minutes to THINK with your partner about what would be the smartest thing to do in this situation.

- Call on pairs of students to share the ideas they came up with. After one pair shares, ask if other students agree with their approach. Encourage lively discussion back and forth. Accept students' ideas without judgment. The most important thing we're going for here is that the students are <u>thinking</u> about the best thing to do in these situations. As the year goes on and students learn more skills, they will see more possibilities and be better able to evaluate their options.

Repeat this procedure with other situations.

Situation 1	Person A plays him- or herself. Person B is Person A's younger brother or sister. Person A is watching TV, and the younger sibling keeps turning off the TV, laughing, joking, trying to make a game of annoying Person A. Person A is getting angrier and angrier. S/he feels like yelling at her sibling or smacking him/her. BUT Person A uses Plan 1-2-3 instead.
Situation 2	Person B plays him- or herself. Both of you are on the playground. Person B is playing tag with some friends. All of a sudden a kick ball comes out of nowhere and hits Person B in the head. The blow hurts and makes Person B angry. S/he finds out that Person A kicked the ball. Person B feels like taking the ball and throwing it as hard as s/he can at Person A's head. BUT, Person B uses Plan 1-2-3 instead.

Evaluation and Closing

Back in the circle, send the talking piece around for students to share their thoughts about Plan 1-2-3. Can they see themselves using it in real life? Why? Why not?

End with a round of applause for their hard work on this challenging topic.

Additional Activities

Cloudy and Clear

You can make a visual aid to explain how abdominal breathing can help settle the mind. Take a clear plastic jar, spoon, water, and clean sand. Show the class a clear jar full of water and ask whether they can see to the other side. Then pour in some clean sand and stir vigorously with a spoon. Ask the students whether they can see to the other side of the jar now. While the sand is stirred up, the water will become cloudy, making it impossible to see through the jar. Then ask students to watch while the sand gradually settles to the bottom of the jar. Ask what they notice. They will likely say that the water is now clear again. Explain that the thoughts and feelings that fill our minds, especially when we are angry or afraid, can be like the sand in the water. These thoughts can make it hard to think clearly. Abdominal breathing can help our thoughts and feelings to "settle down," so that we can think clearly and be more aware of what is happening inside and around us.

This can also be demonstrated with a snow globe or other similar object.

What is peace?

Write the word "peace" in the middle of a piece of chart paper and draw a circle around it. Ask the students what comes to mind when they think of peace. Record their responses, creating a web. You are collecting their free associations. There are no wrong answers. Add your free associations as well. Your web might look something like this:

Ask the students how they would define the word "peace." Elicit that peace is a state of happiness and well-being, free of violence and hurting. We often think of peace as being quiet or calm, but it doesn't have to be. Peace can be exciting and fun. But it's a time when you're in harmony with yourself and others.

Drawing a peaceful place

Ask the students to close their eyes and recall a place they went or something they did that was peaceful. Model thinking of such a place for the students by sharing your memory of a peaceful time or place. Maybe it was a picnic with your family by a beautiful pond when everyone had a great time. Maybe it was a walk by yourself in the park. Give your students a minute or two to think of their own peaceful time or place. Ask them to give you a "thumbs-up" when they have thought of something. Encourage students who haven't thought of something yet. Tell them that if a memory of a peaceful time or place is not coming to mind, they can try to imagine a place they could go or something they could do that would be peaceful.

Distribute crayons and drawing paper and explain that you want them to create an art work that expresses their peaceful place or time. It might be a drawing that shows the place or the activity. Or it might be a design that expresses how they feel in their peaceful place or activity. They should leave room at the bottom of the paper for a sentence of two of explanation.

When they've completed their art works and captions, ask them to pair up and present their work to their partners. Ask a couple of volunteers to share with the group.

Post their completed work on a bulletin board or on the wall above your Peace Corner. (See below.)

Creating a Peace Corner in your classroom

Explain that you want the students' help in making a place in the classroom where they can go for a few minutes to relax if they are upset about something. The Peace Corner will not be a place where a student is sent for a "time out." Going to the Peace Corner will be completely voluntary. A good book for introducing students to the idea of a Peace Corner is *A Quiet Place* by Douglas Wood.

Have a space in mind that you and the class can turn into a little nook with a clear identity, distinct from the rest of the classroom. It should include a small table or desk and a blank wall above the desk that can be decorated with children's art. On the wall above the desk should be a beautiful sign, made by students, naming the space as the "Peace Corner."

Have the class brainstorm ideas of what might go into the Peace Corner, for example, paper and pencils for writing, crayons and paper for drawing, books about feelings, coloring books, a Hugg-A-Planet, a chart with the steps of Plan 1-2-3, photos of beautiful things from nature, a snow globe to remind students of the Cloudy and Clear activity, etc.

Involve the class in making ground rules for the use of the Peace Corner, for example,

- Ask the teacher's permission to go to the Peace Corner
- Return to your regular classroom activities as soon as you feel ready
- Take yourself to a peaceful place
- Use Plan 1-2-3 to cool yourself down

With the students' help, set up the Peace Corner and see how it works!

Make time for silence

During this time the lights are off. No writing, drawing, reading, no gadgets. Just sitting. Encourage students to put their hands on their knees. Students can close their eyes if they want. You can tell them that they can let their minds use the silence as they wish. Or you can suggest ways they might use the silence. For example,

- Practice abdominal breathing
- Simply pay attention to your breathing
- Pay attention to sounds you hear
- In your mind, take yourself to a peaceful place
- Recall a time you had fun
- Recall something you like to do

After the time of silence, ask for a couple of volunteers to share where their minds went during the time. Make time for silence every day, preferably at the same time, such as after lunch or recess or the first and last actions of the day.

By giving students the opportunity to experience time for silence on a daily basis, you'll be instilling a habit that will serve them well for the rest of their lives.

Writing (drawing for younger students) is an excellent way to reinforce and consolidate learning. A journal enables students to put all of their Book Talk writing in one place. You can also give them a few minutes after each 4Rs lesson to jot down a few thoughts about what they're taking away or how they're planning to use what they've just learned. If a student tries a new skill, s/he might want to write about what happened. Did it bring a positive result? If a student is stuck in a conflict with someone, s/he might want to do some writing to sort it out and imagine some solutions. You can give them standard journals and encourage them to decorate them.

By having students keep journals, you will be introducing them to a habit or practice that can serve them well the rest of their lives.

Related Books

The Courage of Sarah Noble by Alice Dalgliesh

The Flunking of Joshua T Bates by Susan Shreve

The Journal of Joshua Loper: A Black Cowboy (My Name Is America) by Walter Dean Myer

Mieko and the Fifth Treasure by Eleanor Coerr

Sadako and the Thousand Paper Cranes by Eleanor Coerr

Sheila Rae the Brave by Kevin Henkes

Stone Fox by John Reynolds Gardiner, illustrated by Marcia Sewall

Handout 1 • Unit 2

If You're Happy and You Know It

If you're happy and you know it, clap your hands
If you're happy and you know it, clap your hands
If you're happy and you know it and you really want to show it,
If you're happy and you know it, clap your hands.

If you're sad and you know it, go "boo hoo"

If you're tired you know it, yawn like this (*yawn, yawn*)

If you're nervous and you know it, shake like this (*shake, shake*)

If you're angry and you know it, stomp your feet

And an alternative verse for "angry" more in keeping with The 4Rs:
If you're angry and you know it, take a breath (*breathe, breathe*)

With the students, make up verses for other feelings.

Handout 2 ♦ Unit 2

"I Whistle a Happy Tune"
from *The King and I* by Richard Rodgers and Oscar Hammerstein II

"Whenever I feel afraid
I hold my head erect
And whistle a happy tune,
So no one will suspect
I'm afraid.

While shivering in my shoes
I strike a careless pose
And whistle a happy tune,
And no one ever knows
I'm afraid.

The result of this deception
Is very strange to tell,
For when I fool the people I fear
I fool myself as well!

I whistle a happy tune,
And every single time
The happiness in the tune
Convinces me that I'm
Not afraid!

Make believe you're brave
And the trick will take you far;
You may be as brave
As you make believe you are.
You may be as brave
As you make believe you are."

"I Whistle A Happy Tune" by Richard Rodgers and Oscar Hammerstein II
Copyright © 1951 by Richard Rodgers and Oscar Hammerstein II
Copyright Renewed.

WILLIAMSON MUSIC owner of publication and allied rights throughout the world.

International Copyright Secured.   All Rights Reserved.   Used by Permission.

Grade 3 · JoJo's Flying Side Kick

Handout 3 ♦ Unit 2

Triggers and Self-Talk

Choose one of your triggers — for fear, anger, or nervousness. Write it below. Then think of something you might say to yourself to calm yourself down when you are triggered in this way.

One of my triggers is

_____

_____

Here is what I might say to myself

_____

_____

Blank by design.

3

Unit 3 Theme

Becoming a Better Listener

Unit 3 Book Selection

The Pain and the Great One by Judy Blume
Atheneum Books for Young Readers, 2014

Activities

- Intro to active listening: The Three Ps
- The First P: paying good attention
- The Second P: providing gentle encouragement
- The Third P: paraphrasing
- Introducing the concept of conflict
- Writing about conflict
- Role-play: Point of view
- Additional Activities

Introduction

Therapists call it "listening with the third ear"; folk adages warn that children "learn from what you do, not what you say," or that "Actions speak louder than words"; Native Americans urge that we not judge another until we have walked in that person's moccasins. No matter how you say it, the message is clear. Communication is more than one person speaking and another listening. Two people may hear the same words, but each understands them through filters of culture and experience. In addition, tone of voice, body language, what is said or not said, give information about what people are thinking and feeling.

The ability to listen well and to understand another person's point of view is crucial to conflict resolution. In any human interaction (and, by extension, any conflict) each person has his or her own point of view. I can like chocolate ice cream and you can like vanilla, but if my point of view is that people who like vanilla have no taste we could end up in conflict. Many people make the mistake of thinking that their point of view is the norm and therefore, that the solution to any conflict with another will involve that person or group coming around to their point of view. In fact, if there is a solution, it lies in finding common ground, not in changing deeply held beliefs or cultural conditioning.

Before we can understand another's point of view, we must be good listeners. A good listener takes in information, interprets it, draws conclusions about what the person is saying, and uses all this to try to understand what is going on. Being able to put one's own mind into another's as much as possible makes for better listening. The better the listening, the more accurate the analysis and the more useful the response.

One could argue that listening well to people is the key to conflict resolution. In our own era, we have seen the Truth Commissions in South Africa, where victims of apartheid are able to tell their stories. Their pain and losses cannot be undone, but the government hopes that by promoting the telling of stories and good listening, it can help heal the nation's wounds and reduce the desire for vengeance.

> **GOOD LISTENING**
> - shows respect for (and interest in) the other person
> - helps avoid misunderstanding
> - helps clear up misunderstandings if they occur
> - gives us important information about how the other person is thinking and feeling
> - can help defuse anger
> - can help us develop and improve our thinking
>
> **COMMUNICATION BARRIERS**
> - blaming the other person
> - using put-downs
> - ignoring the other person's concerns
> - offering solutions too early
> - not taking the other person's concerns seriously
> - thinking only of our own ideas
> - interrupting

Listening is a skill that can be learned. We believe not only that good listening is essential in dealing well with conflict, but that we can all improve our skills and become better listeners. Although listening is part of every unit, it is the special focus of this unit. Students at all grade levels practice a set of skills called "active listening." Active listening has three main components: paying good attention, providing gentle encouragement (to the speaker), and restating or reflecting to the speaker what we've heard (to show our interest and check our understanding).

GOOD LISTENING CHECKLIST

- positive body language
- eye contact
- no interrupting

We also help students to understand the concept of point of view and its relationship to literature and to conflict resolution. It is because each of us has our own point of view that good listening is so critical. We can't assume that others see things as we do. If we truly want to respect other people, we often have to work hard to understand where they're coming from.

In this unit

	Ideas	Skills
Literacy	• Stories have characters • One character can tell the story (first-person narration) • Sometimes we can use stories to understand our own lives • Writers can use rhymes and repetition to make the story interesting • Words and pictures together can tell a story	• Predicting • Identifying the main idea • Asking questions • Expressing ideas clearly • Providing evidence to back up one's assertions • Listening
Social and Emotional Learning	• Listening is a key to solving conflicts • Listening can help us be less angry • Listening can help us think better	• Listening well • Using words to communicate with others • Taking initiative • Developing positive body language

The Pain and the Great One, by Judy Blume.
Illustrated by Debbie Ridpath Ohi. Atheneum Books for Young Readers, 2014. Text c. 1974, Illustrations c. 2014

SUMMARY

This book is really two in one. First we read about the Pain, a six-year-old boy who, according to his third-grade sister, gets to do whatever he wants and is their parents' favorite. She complains that he won't get out of bed in the morning and has to be carried into the kitchen, as well as helped to dress. When she tries to leave without him, he cries and their mother yells at her. The parents ooh and aah over his schoolwork, let him have dessert even if he hasn't finished the main course, and don't seem to be upset when he makes messes. When she complains that he shouldn't stay up as late as she does, they agree and put him to bed. But the evening is not as exciting as she had hoped; the parents do not pay attention to her. She decides to go to bed, because "without the Pain / There's nothing to do! Remember that tomorrow," her mother says. Nevertheless, the next day brings another litany of grievances, until she ends with the plaint, "I think they love him better than me."

In the next section, entitled "The Great One," we get the brother's point of view. He thinks she's a "jerk" who considers herself superior just because she can do so many more things than he can, such as use the telephone, open the cat food, hold a baby cousin, and play the piano. He resents her having friends over to play with blocks, which occasionally he knocks down in his capacity as garbage man. The parents agree that he should have the blocks to himself for a while. He builds a whole country, but "it's not the funnest thing / To play blocks alone. . . . 'Remember that tomorrow,'" says his mother. At the beach, his resentment over his sister's ability to swim and dive boils over when she calls him a baby because he's scared to put his face in the water. The conflict quickly escalates as he spits water at her, pulls her hair, and even pinches her "sometimes" in response to the name-calling. His last thought is, "I think they love her better than me."

COMMENT

The humorous drawings and the easy-to-read text written as a prose poem draw the reader into a story of sibling rivalry that reflects universal experiences of misunderstanding and feeling misunderstood. We can ask what would happen if the characters ever actually listened to each other. We can look at how each one escalates conflicts. The parents are accommodating and understanding, but seem to yell a lot; and although they are aware of the sibling bond that ties the Pain and the Great One, they do nothing to encourage communication. Instead, they agree to let each child engage in a favorite activity alone, then count on the resulting boredom to bring the children closer together. Where some parents might try to spend time alone with each child in order to allay jealousy, they are content with crisis management. We can ask if their strategies are good ones and what else they could do? We can notice how the author describes the same situation from different perspectives and encourage the students to do the same. We can note the way that the sentences are laid out like a prose poem rather than a straight narrative. We can note the parallel structures and themes of the text.

Grade 3   The Pain and the Great One

Book Talk

READ ALOUD

Previewing the book

Look at the cover of the book. Ask the students to tell everything they notice about the drawing. What do they think the book will be about? Who are the main characters? Can they guess which character is which? Read the dedication. What does this tell us? Has anyone read other books by this author?

Reading and responding to the text

Read the story.

After reading the story, ask the students to pair up and talk about the book. What interests them? What questions do they have? Ask students to share their questions and comments with the class. Encourage as much class participation as possible by asking questions such as, "Do the rest of you agree or disagree with _____?" If others want to respond to a comment from one student, suggest that they restate in their own words what the child has said, then give their opinion and their reasons.

Deepening the students' understanding of the book

Ask if the students have noticed anything about the way the words are placed on the page? This book is written like a prose poem, a poem that does not rhyme and that uses regular sentences. What reasons could the author have for using this form?

Introduce the idea that this book describes several conflicts. Say that a conflict is a disagreement, argument, or fight. Conflicts often start out small and build up. One person says something. The other person gets mad and says something back. The first person gets even madder and says or does something that makes the conflict worse. In this book there are many places where something starts out as a small irritation and builds to a bigger conflict. Say that you will read the book again and this time you want the students to notice all the places where the conflicts get worse, or escalate.

For example, on p. 4, the brother is slow to get dressed and his sister wants to catch the bus. She walks out, evoking cries from the brother. This makes her mother yell at her. Now she is even madder at her brother. Have students lived through scenes like this with siblings or friends? Can they describe the back and forth reactions that escalate the conflict?

The narrator escalates her grievances in her own mind, continuing to be irritated by his table manners, his bathing habits, and his bedtime. Has anyone ever had the experience of holding feelings in and then having them build up and come out in an angry way?

Part of the narrator's point of view is that her parents "love him better than me." Do the students think this is true? Why? Why not? Ask for evidence from the book.

The 4Rs © Morningside Center for Teaching Social Responsibility

After p. 17, we get the brother's point of view. He, too, has a long list of complaints. One, on p. 26, is, "My sister thinks she's so great / Just because she can / Remember phone numbers. And when she dials / She never gets / The wrong person." Does anyone remember a time when they had trouble dialing a phone number? What was it like?

On p. 35, we see the conflict escalating: "Which is why / I have to spit water at her / And pull her hair / And even pinch her sometimes." Is it true that he *has* to do these things to her? Why? Why not?

He also thinks, "they love her better than me." Do the students think this is true?

Ask, what are some of the big ideas this book deals with? What are things this story seems to be saying that are important to you? What do we think the author was trying to do in this book? Draw out the students' ideas. Bring up the idea that the author appears to be saying that people have conflicts when they have different points of view. Explore this idea with the students. Do they agree that brothers and sisters or close friends have different points of view? Is conflict, therefore, inevitable? Can they or their parents do anything to deal better with the conflicts?

Make a T-chart and put Pain in one column and Great One in another. List aspects of each character's point of view (mad at brother for messing up bathroom, mad at sister for being allowed to hold the baby).

Students may notice that in the family portrayed in the book, mornings are tough. As the sister worries about missing the bus, she raises what is already a high-tension situation by trying to leave without her brother. Later, although the conflicts are not described, we see escalating behavior as the brother makes noise while his sister is on the phone and drives into her construction when she is using building blocks. He is fearful of the water, she teases him, and he retaliates by spitting water at her, pulling her hair, and pinching her. There are other situations that are conflicts waiting to happen, such as at the dinner table, around child care of the cousin, and feeding the cat.

Ask the class for suggestions of things the brother and sister could do to de-escalate the conflicts. Is there anything the parents could have done?

Connecting the book to students' lives

Discussion: It's very common for people to feel that somebody else is getting all the attention from a parent or teacher or another student. Have you ever felt that somebody else was getting attention you wanted? This person may have been older or younger than you. Pair up and tell your partner about how you felt about this person. Now think about what that person's point of view might have been. Tell that point of view to your partner. (Throughout The 4Rs curriculum, there are partner discussions such as this that may bring up strong emotions. Consider suggesting to students that they take a few abdominal breaths before and after speaking, as a way of managing feelings, cooling down and thinking more clearly, and listening with greater presence and attention to the other person.)

Have you ever had a conflict with an older or younger person? Describe the conflict to your partner. Did the conflict escalate? Can you describe how it escalated? Can you think of something you could have done to de-escalate it? Can you think of something you wish the other person had done to de-escalate the conflict?

Writing: Ask the class to write in their own words one scene in the book. However, change the scene so that the brother and sister prevent or work out a conflict.

Review the elements of dialogue in writing (two or more people talking to each other) and ask each student to write a dialogue for two or three people who are having a conflict over something silly and don't listen to each other as they escalate the conflict. They can make it funny. Ask students to share their dialogues if they wish and break them into groups to act them out in front of the class. What did the class learn about conflict? Who was "right"?

The book we just read was a prose poem. We can make prose poems by taking vivid sentences and rearranging them on a page. Ask students to write a sentence about a conflict they had with a sibling or friend. Ask for volunteers to read their sentences. Arrange the words on the chalkboard so that it looks like a poem. Then ask the other students to do the same with their sentence. For example, "My brother always wants to ride my bike and this time I let him and he scraped the bright blue paint."

> My brother
> always
> wants to ride
> my bike
>
> and this time
> I let him
>
> and he scraped
> the bright blue
> paint.

ROLE-PLAY

Divide the class into groups of three or four and ask them to act out two scenes from the book—one from the point of view of the brother and the other from the point of view of the sister. Present the scenes to the class.

Unit 3: ListeningGrade 3

Applied Learning

Lesson 1

Objectives

Students will
- learn and practice a simple classroom ritual for good listening;
- identify the "three Ps" of Active Listening;
- practice the first "P": paying good attention;
- practice the second "P": providing gentle encouragement.

Materials Needed

- agenda on chart paper or the chalkboard

Gathering: Go-Round

Introduce the idea of a "Go-Round" by passing a simple gesture around the group, such as a wave or a "high-five." Turn to the student on your right, pass the gesture, and tell that student to turn to her/his right and pass it to a second student. Go around until everyone has had a turn. Then explain that this time, you will send a question around the circle for each person to answer.

What's your favorite color? Each child takes a turn to answer this question in the following way: "My name is _____ and my favorite color is _____."

When everyone takes a turn speaking, we call it a "go-round." Go-rounds should be used sparingly, because children tend to get restless waiting for all of their classmates to speak. Make sure the question you use in a go-round calls for a short, simple answer. Tell the children that they can pass if they want to.

Take the opportunity of today's go-round to introduce a simple classroom practice for talking and listening, and give the children a chance to practice it. You can use an object like a Hugg-A-Planet or a "talking stick." The child who is speaking holds the object. Only the child holding it can speak, while all of the others give that child their full attention.

Check agenda

Go over the objectives and the agenda.

Introduction to Active Listening: The Three Ps

Remind the children that listening is an important skill in dealing with conflict. Many unnecessary conflicts can be avoided if people listen well, treat each other with respect, and try to understand where the other person is coming from. When we have a conflict, listening is one of the best ways to work toward a solution. We are listening all time — we listen to television, to noise on the street, to people talking. One of our goals in this class is to learn and practice a special kind of listening called "active listening." To help children remember the sets of skills that make up active listening, we can say that it consists of

The Three Ps

Paying good attention

Providing gentle encouragement

Paraphrasing and reflecting back what we hear

By practicing the Three Ps, we show respect for the other person, we can learn from them, we can understand where they are coming from.

The First P: Paying Good Attention

Say that in this activity, we'll review "Good and Poor Listening" (Unit 1, page 9) and create lists of listening Dos and Don'ts. We'll focus especially on the "First P," paying good attention.

Ask for a volunteer to come up and talk about something s/he likes to do. Model paying good attention and ask the children to watch you closely. After the child is done talking, ask the children to identify specific behaviors of yours that represented paying good attention (for example, you were facing the child, you sat down so you were more on his level, you had a smile on your face, you looked right at him). Record those behaviors on a T-chart under Good Listening Dos.

Then with an imaginary child in the chair, act out a number of poor listening behaviors (for example, a frown on your face, looking at your watch, moving around in your chair). Ask the children to identify these negative behaviors and record them on the T-chart as Listening Don'ts.

Then reverse roles: ask a child to come up and demonstrate paying good attention while you tell about something you like to do. Ask the class to notice the behaviors the child used.

Then have a child to come up and demonstrate poor listening behaviors while you talk. Ask the children to identify those behaviors.

Finally, ask the children to pair up. One child speaks about something s/he likes to do on the weekend for one minute while the other child gives good attention (by showing good listening behaviors). Then they switch roles and repeat the activity.

Afterward, discuss: how did it feel when someone paid good attention to you? How was it to be the listener? Easy? Difficult? All of us, whether adults or children, need reminders to keep our listening at its best. So give the children ample opportunities to practice paying good attention, one of the key aspects of active listening.

Unit 3: Listening   Grade 3

The Second P: Providing Gentle Encouragement

Tell the children that another part of active listening, the "Second P," is providing gentle encouragement. You can do this by simply saying, "Tell me more" or "I'd like to hear more about that." You can also ask questions. When you ask a question, you show you're interested in what the other person is saying. We often ask questions when we don't understand something or when we want to know more. In school, if you don't understand something the teacher says, it's important to ask a question. If you don't, you may miss some important directions or some important information.

Have the children practice asking questions by telling them a simple story about something that happened to you recently and pausing to encourage them to ask you a question about your story — either something they want to know more about or something they don't understand. Reverse roles: Ask a child to come up and talk about a favorite pet and model asking gentle questions to get the person to say more.

Then ask the children to talk in pairs about a favorite pet or their favorite animal and say that in this exercise, in addition to paying good attention, you want them to ask a question of the other person. After the first child has had a turn to talk and answer the other child's question, they switch and the other child gets a chance to talk.

Evaluation

What's one thing you learned today about one of your classmates that you didn't know before? Give several volunteers a chance to tell the class.

Closing: Moment of Silence

Tell the children you want them to close their eyes and become completely still. When they are completely quiet, you want them to listen very well. Do they hear anything? If so, what are the sounds? Where are they coming from?

After a minute or two of "silence," ask them what sounds, if any, they heard. What do they think was making each of the sounds they heard? Why do they think so?

A variation on the "Moment of Silence" is to strike a chime or ring a bell and ask students to listen with their eyes closed. When they can no longer hear the sound of the chime, they can raise their hands. How long does it take before the sound can no longer be heard? *(You can order inexpensive chimes online. Or, the music teacher may have a chime or bells you can borrow. Apps for chimes or bells can also be downloaded onto smartphones.)*

Another alternative is to do this with recorded music. Gradually lower the volume until the sound is inaudible and students raise their hands.)

Lesson 2

Objectives

Students will:
- practice the skill of paraphrasing
- sharpen their powers of observation

Materials Needed

- agenda on chart paper or the chalkboard

Gathering: Clap and Repeat

Clap out a simple rhythm, or tap a rhythm on a small drum. Ask the students to respond by clapping out the same rhythm in unison. As the activity progresses, rhythms may become longer and more complex. Students can also be invited to take turns leading the "Clap and Repeat." Continue for as long as interest remains high. This builds listening skills, and a sense of community.

Check agenda

Go over the objectives and the agenda.

The Third P: Paraphrasing

Tell the children that another part of active listening, the "Third P," is paraphrasing: saying back in your own words what someone has said. Model it by asking for a volunteer to come up and talk about his or her favorite sport or game. After the child has spoken for a minute or so, paraphrase what the child said. Then reverse roles and ask the child to paraphrase what you say. Point out that that unlike the "Clap and Repeat" activity, paraphrasing is not simply repetition.

Then give the children a chance to practice in pairs. Keep the time for them: one minute for the speaker to talk while the listener listens; another minute or so for the listener to paraphrase; another minute or less for the speaker to correct the paraphrase or add anything s/he wants to add. After the exercise is finished, ask the listeners how it was to listen and paraphrase. Was it easy? Difficult? If so, how? Then ask the speakers how they felt having someone pay good attention and then paraphrase what they'd said. Point out that paraphrasing is a key skill in mediation—where a third person helps two disputants talk out a conflict they're having. (Children may be familiar with mediation by having a peer mediation program in their school.)

Evaluation

What's one thing you learned from today's lesson?

Unit 3: Listening   Grade 3

Closing: New Millennium Telephone Game

Begin with the traditional game in which you whisper a sentence to the child next to you who whispers it to the child next to him and so on all around the circle. Do it once in the traditional way. Then tell the children you'll play the game again but this time they should use active listening. In other words, they should pay good attention, ask a question if they aren't sure they've heard correctly, and restate what they've heard to be sure they got it. The message should come through much better this time.

Lesson 3

Objectives

Students will
- define the word "conflict";
- share times they were involved in a conflict;
- write about conflicts.

Materials Needed

- agenda on chart paper or the chalkboard
- paper and pencil for writing

Gathering: Changes

Part of good listening is being a keen observer. To sharpen children's powers of observation, introduce the game "Changes." The children work in pairs. One child closes and covers his eyes while the other turns around and changes three things about himself. (He might take off his glasses, tuck in his shirt, change his watch from one wrist to the other.) When he turns back around, the other child opens his eyes and tries to identify the three changes. Then they switch.

Check agenda

Go over the objectives and the agenda.

Introducing the concept of conflict

In *The Pain and the Great One*, the brother and sister have many conflicts. The word conflict was introduced in Book Talk. Here we develop the idea further.

Write the word conflict in the middle of the chalkboard or a large piece of chart paper. Ask the children to say words that come to their minds when they hear the word "conflict." Write the words on the board or chart paper and connect them with lines to the word "conflict" to form a web.

Below is a typical "conflict web."

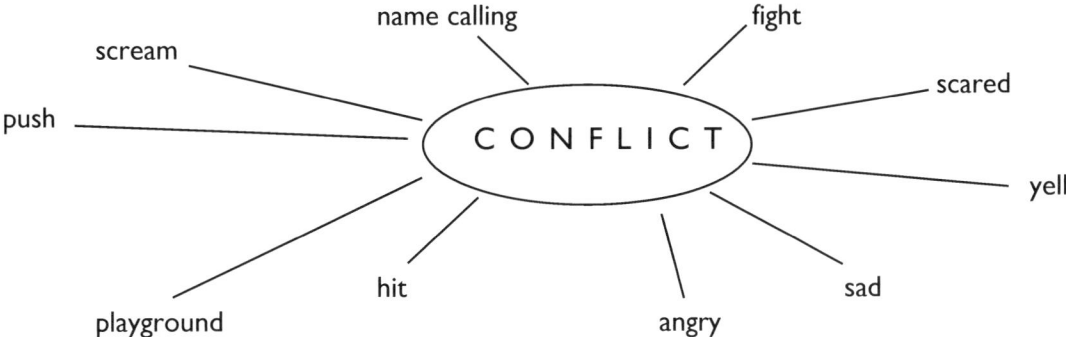

Ask the children if they have anything they want to say about the web. What do they notice? Most conflict webs, whether made by children or adults, consist primarily of negative words. The children may notice this. If they don't (and if it's true of your web), point it out. Explain that people see conflict as something bad because they tend to link it with violence, with people hurting other people. Conflict can lead to violence sometimes, but it doesn't have to, especially if people have the skills we're developing through the 4Rs curriculum.

Jumping off from the web, develop with the class a working definition of "conflict" as an argument, a disagreement, or a fight. Ask the class to recall some of the conflicts between the brother and sister in the story. There are many kinds of conflicts. Friends can argue over what they want to do together during free time. Classmates can argue over who gets to go first on the computer. This is normal. We all have conflicts from time to time. Conflict is part of life. Ask for volunteers to share with the class a time when they had a conflict. Elicit a few conflict stories from the class.

Writing about conflict

Once you're sure the class understands the concept, have them do a writing activity. Ask them to write about a time they had a conflict. Suggest that their pieces include the following (not necessarily in this order):

- Who was involved in the conflict?
- Where did it take place?
- How were you feeling? How were other people feeling? How did you and the other people express their feelings?
- What caused the conflict?
- What happened? How did it turn out? Was the conflict resolved?
- Were you happy with the way it came out?

Give the students 20-30 minutes to write, then ask them to share their writing with a partner. Remind them to use their good listening skills in paying attention to the other person's piece. They should feel free to use the Second P (Provide Gentle Encouragement) if they want to know more. They can also practice taking a few abdominal breaths before sharing, to help them stay focused on the speaker.

After the students have read their pieces to each other in pairs, ask for several volunteers to read their pieces to the group.

Discuss: Was it helpful to write about a conflict? Did writing lead to any insights that will help you deal with this conflict or with a similar conflict in the future?

Evaluation

What's one new idea that you're taking away from this lesson? Give several volunteers a chance to share their thoughts.

Closing: Stretches

Have the children stand up and tell them you're going to lead in them doing "stretches." Make sure there's enough room between each child. "First we stretch up." Put your arms straight up over your head and reach for the ceiling. "Now we stretch down." Bend over and touch your toes. "Now we stretch right." With your arms outstretched, bend at the waist and stretch to the right. "Now we stretch to the left." With your arms outstretched, bend at the waist and stretch to the left. And so on.

Lesson 4

Objectives

Students will
- role-play situations in which characters have different points of view;
- identify the problem and the feelings the characters are having;
- coach the characters in solving the problems.

Materials Needed

- agenda on chart paper or the chalkboard

Gathering: Louder/Softer

Explain that we all speak in different volumes at different times and places. Ask the students to say or sing the sound "Ahhh" in unison with you, using a normal "indoor voice." Then explain that you will use hand gestures to change the volume, in the way that you would raise or lower the volume on a television, computer, radio, or other device students are familiar with. When your hand is at about chest height, students can use an "indoor voice" volume. When your hand is extended as far over your head as it will go, that is an "outdoor voice" or "playground voice" volume. When your hand is lowered as far as it will go, that is a "whispering" volume. Raise and lower your hand several times to raise and lower the volume of the sound that students are making. Vary the speed at which you raise and lower your hand to encourage the students to focus on observing your hand movements.

Grade 3 — The Pain and the Great One

Check agenda

Go over the objectives and the agenda.

Role-play (Point of View)

In a conflict, each person has his or her own point of view. We saw this clearly in *The Pain and the Great One*. In Book Talk, the class worked to understand the sister's point of view and the brother's. In this activity, we further develop the children's understanding of "point of view." The teacher presents role-plays in which the characters come into conflict and have different points of view on the situation. The children try to understand where the characters are coming from and coach them about solutions to the problem.

Situation 1

The teacher plays a mother, and a child volunteer plays a child. Feel free to improvise on the script below.

Mother:	Clean up your room now.
Child:	I'm tired, Mom. I don't want to do it right now.
Mother:	It's like a pig pen. Dirty dishes, piles of dirty clothes on the floor. It'll attract roaches and germs. You'll get sick.
Child:	No I won't, Mom. You're exaggerating. Anyway, I'll clean it. Just not now. I'm tired.
Mother:	There's always some excuse. Either you're tired or too busy. Meanwhile, the room gets messier and messier.
Child:	Mom, I wish you'd stop nagging me.

Pause the action. Ask, What is happening here? How do you think the characters are feeling? What's the point of view of the mother? The point of view of the child? Who do you think is right? Elicit children's thinking. Point out that there isn't always a clear right or wrong in an argument. What do they agree with the mother about? What do they agree with the child about?

What advice would you give them for resolving their conflict?

Have you ever experienced a conflict like this? How did it turn out?

Situation 2

The teacher plays Ms. Brown, a teacher, and a child volunteer plays Joanna, a third grader. Feel free to improvise on the script.

Ms. Brown:	Joanna, can I speak to you for a moment.
Joanna:	Sure. *[The two go to the teacher's desk to have a private conversation.]*
Ms. Brown:	I've decided to change your seat so you're not sitting next to Yvonne.

Joanna:	Why? Yvonne's my best friend! We always sit together — ever since we've been in this school.
Ms. Brown:	I know. That's the problem. The two of you are always talking.
Joanna:	But all of the talking we do is about our work. You know that Yvonne has trouble with reading and math. I'm helping her. She depends on me.
Ms. Brown:	I'm afraid she's depending on you too much. She counts on you for the answers and that's keeping her from thinking for herself. Also, I know you don't only talk about your work.
Joanna:	I never give her the answers. I ask questions. I make her think it out for herself. Why don't you ask Yvonne what she thinks? Please don't split us up! We're best friends!
Ms. Brown:	I'm sorry, but I just don't think it's working.

Pause the action and model using Plan 1-2-3, "Stop-Breathe-Think" (Unit 2, Lesson 4, p. 31), Guide the class in understanding the points of view of both characters, as you did above. Again, point out that in a conflict there's not always a clear-cut right or wrong. Where do you think Ms. Brown might have a point? Where do you think Joanna might have a point? What advice would you give them for resolving their conflict so that both of them (and Yvonne) feel good about it?

Situation 3

Get volunteers from the class to play two children, Michael and Jason.

Michael:	Let's work at the computer.
Jason:	No, I'd rather play with the Legos. We could build a city together.
Michael:	Oh, come on. Legos are baby stuff. We could do some cool stuff with the computer. I'll show you.
Jason:	Every time we have free time, we do what you want to do. This time I want to do what I want to do. Remember last time you promised that this time it would be my choice.
Michael:	I know, but the computer is never open, and today it is. Finally we have a chance to use it. I don't want to pass up the chance.
Jason:	We agreed this time it would be my choice.

Ask the students to raise their hands at a point in the dialogue where it might be useful to use Plan 1-2-3, "Stop-Breathe-Think". Pause the action here, and guide the children in reflecting on the situation, as above.

Evaluation

What's one thing you liked about today's lesson? Give a few volunteers a chance to share their thoughts.

Closing: Something I'm Looking Forward To

Children talk in pairs for a moment about something they're looking forward to. Ask for a couple of volunteers to share with the group.

Additional Activities

Who's missing?

The children are sitting in a circle in no particular order. A child leaves the room. While she's gone, one or more children hide. The rest of the children close in the circle. When the child comes back, she tries to figure out who's missing.

Conflict Escalator

The students are no doubt familiar with escalators in office buildings or department stores. We can use the idea of the escalator to talk about conflict. When a conflict starts small and then people do things that make them angrier and angrier, we say they are "going up the conflict escalator." If they gradually calm down, we say that they "going down the conflict escalator."

Discuss: Have you ever go up the conflict escalator? When? What happened? Have you ever gone down the conflict escalator? Did someone help you or did you do it yourself?

Ask the students to write a dialogue between two people who are going up the conflict escalator (that is, having a conflict in which they are getting angrier and angrier at each other. Suggest that at a certain point, one of the people in the conflict or a third person intervenes and changes the energy so that the two people start going down the conflict escalator. What does the third person do? What's the dialogue like now that they're going down the escalator?

The "conflict escalator" is a useful idea for understanding conflict situations. Help the children see how it applies in conflicts the children encounter in the 4Rs curriculum, in children's literature, and in real life.

Make time for silence

During this time the lights are off. No writing, drawing, reading, no gadgets. Just sitting. Encourage students to put their hands on their knees. Students can close their eyes if they want. You can tell them that they can let their minds use the silence as they wish. Or you can suggest ways they might use the silence. For example,

- Practice abdominal breathing (introduced in Unit 2)
- Simply pay attention to your breathing
- Pay attention to sounds you hear in your mind, take yourself to a peaceful place
- Recall a time you had fun
- Recall something you like to do

After the time of silence, ask for a couple of volunteers to share where their minds went during the time. Make time for silence every day, preferably at the same time, such as after lunch or recess or the first and last actions of the day.

By giving students the opportunity to experience time for silence on a daily basis, you'll be instilling a habit that will serve them well for the rest of their lives.

Consider having your students keep a 4Rs journal

Writing (drawing for younger students) is an excellent way to reinforce and consolidate learning. A journal enables students to put all of their Book Talk writing in one place. You can also give them a few minutes after each 4Rs lesson to jot down a few thoughts about what they're taking away or how they're planning to use what they've just learned. If a student tries a new skill, s/he might want to write about what happened. Did it bring a positive result? If a student is stuck in a conflict with someone, s/he might want to do some writing to sort it out and imagine some solutions. You can give them standard journals and encourage them to decorate them.

By having students keep journals, you will be introducing them to a habit or practice that can serve them well the rest of their lives.

Related Books

The Blind Men and the Elephant by Karen Blackstein, illustrated by Anne Mitra

Many Moons by James Thurber

The One in the Middle Is the Green Kangaroo by Judy Blume, illustrated by Irene Trivas. (Judy Blume is a prolific writer whose work lends itself to an author study)

Teacher's Pet by Johanna Hurwitz, illustrated by Sheila Hamanaka

Where Butterflies Grow by Joanne Ryder, illustrated by Lynne Cherry

3

Unit 4 Theme

Learning to Be Assertive

Unit 4 Book Selection

Hank Aaron: Brave in Every Way by Peter Golenbock
Gulliver Books, Harcourt, Inc. 2001

Activities

- Choices
- Strong, Mean, and Giving In
- Consequences
- I-Messages
- Draining
- Assertiveness Line
- Additional Activities

Unit 4: Assertiveness — Grade 3

Introduction

Assertive behavior helps us to pursue our needs and protect our space and interests without dominating or abusing others. We can look at assertiveness in the following schema:

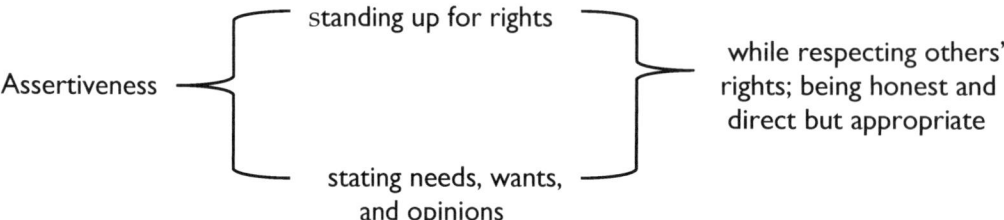

Children see few models of assertive behavior. Too many adults use their unequal power to threaten children. Television, video, and movie characters often act aggressively or respond to aggression with hostile acts. More and more, we see adults and children who can think of no other response to threats (real or imagined) than violence. Children carry weapons to school. Adults are out on the firing range.

Being assertive is a stance toward life. The assertive person is neither victim nor bully. Assertiveness, like active listening, involves a set of skills that can be learned. Students will find assertiveness skills useful in such situations as

- dealing with teasing and bullying
- dealing with peer pressure, saying no to things they don't want to do and putting forth their point of view even when it's not the popular thing to say
- handling issues with friends and family
- asking for what they need
- standing up to injustice

True strength comes from self-knowledge. We can learn how to know ourselves better through reading, reflecting, and writing. How is this character feeling? What do you think the character will do? Have you ever felt this way? What would you do? Using this knowledge, we will be better prepared to make wise choices. We can practice assertiveness skills through group discussions, role-plays, and paired exercises.

In this curriculum, we explore the factors that allow students to develop assertive behavior and present techniques for developing such behavior. In the lower grades, we focus on the basics: saying no and stating needs clearly. In the upper grades, we add additional strategies, such as I-messages, which are useful with people who care about our feelings.

In this unit

	Ideas	Skills
Literacy	• Stories have characters • Sometimes we can use stories to understand our own lives • Words and pictures together can tell a story • Writers often use humor to tell a story	• Summarizing the action • Predicting • Identifying the main idea • Asking questions • Expressing ideas clearly • Providing evidence to back up ones assertions
Social and Emotional Learning	• Friends can be assertive with each other and not destroy the friendship • There are many different ways to respond to any given situation • You can be strong without being mean	• Assertive strategies • Naming feelings • Regulating one's emotions • Staying calm under pressure

Hank Aaron: Brave in Every Way, by Peter Golenbock, illustrated by Paul Lee. Gulliver Books, Harcourt, Inc, 2001.

SUMMARY

The world knows Hank Aaron as the man who broke Babe Ruth's record of home runs and as a great baseball player. But when he was born in 1934, only his parents had high hopes for him. His father "wanted him to know the joy of playing baseball in open grassy fields," and his mother "dreamed that one day he would make a difference in the world." Times were tough. The Great Depression had ravaged the country. Like countless others, Hank's father, Herbert Aaron, had trouble finding work. He saved enough to buy some land outside of Mobile, Alabama, but had no money for a house or even wood to build one. When Hank was eight years old his dad used boards from a torn-down house to build a small home with no electricity, glass windows, or indoor plumbing. But the elder Aaron had achieved a major goal. Not only had he provided a home for his family, he built it near "an open field for playing ball."

Young Hank loved playing ball. His mother wanted him to go to college. "Hank, try to be the best....Set goals for yourself and don't let anyone stop you from achieving them." Hank studied, but he also played ball. His goal, which seemed impossible at the time, was to be a major-league ballplayer. His father urged him to be realistic: "There aren't any colored players in the major leagues." Hank didn't stop dreaming, and when he turned 13, Jackie Robinson broke the color bar by joining the Brooklyn Dodgers.

At age 16, Hank was offered a job with a local team called the Black Bears. The Bears would pay him ten dollars a game. Hank thought he would have a conflict with his mother. Not only were the other Bears adults, but the team played games on Sunday. He was sure she would say no. Still, he wanted to play with the Bears more than anything. He "put his fears away and asked permission." To his surprise, his mother came up with a win-win solution. He had to stay in school and get his diploma. She wouldn't let him travel with the team or be paid on Sunday, but he could play in all the home games. After two seasons with the Black Bears, he got an offer from a professional team called the Indianapolis Clowns. "Be strong," his mother cautioned as she bid him farewell, too "upset to go to the train station to see him off." And he would need strength. His talent led him to the Milwaukee Braves. He had achieved his goal to play in the major leagues. He became one of the leading home run hitters in the country. Now he set himself another goal: to break the career home run record of Babe Ruth, "baseball's most beloved hero."

When the Braves moved from Milwaukee to Atlanta, Georgia, the hate mail started arriving. Meanwhile, Hank was making steady progress toward the goal he had set for himself in the late 1950s. It was 1972, and he was 41 runs away from Ruth's total of 714 home runs. The hate mail intensified. Many people did not want an African American to do better than a white man. "Hank decided to fight the best way he could. He swore that each angry letter would add a home run to his record."

As word of the hate mail and death threats got out, well-wishers sent letters, too. A "whole country of fans cheered for him." On the day in 1974 when he hit 715, both his parents were in the stands. His mother feared for his life. What if someone tried to keep him from reaching home base? When he *got to home base, she threw her arms around him and held on very tight. Her dream that her child would make a difference had been achieved.*

COMMENT

There is a saying that we stand on the shoulders of those who went before us. Hank Aaron always acknowledged his debt to Jackie Robinson and others whose courage and assertiveness paved the way for him and many others. Peter Golenbock has written about Robinson and the intense racial hatred he faced from his own teammates as well as from fans. We can look at his book *Teammates*, which chronicles Robinson's story and the support he received from one white teammate who was courageous enough to transcend his own southern upbringing and also stand up to racist whites on his team. Both books take us back to a time that is ancient history for our students. It may be hard for them to imagine a time when African Americans were not major league players; when teams could have names like Black Bears and Indianapolis Clowns; when the slightest show of assertion by an African American could lead to death. This book is also in the tradition of stories of the American dream. The hero may not have been born in a log cabin, but the outlines of the tale remain the same.

We can look at the quiet courage and assertiveness of the entire Aaron family. In the midst of very hard economic times the father never loses sight of his desire to make a home for his family and to own land when so many families were in thrall to white landowners. His mother continues to believe in the power of education. She stays true to her faith, finding a way for her son to work on her dream without compromising the values she has instilled in him. Hank works unceasingly toward his goals, first to join the major leagues, then to break Babe Ruth's record. He does this without demeaning himself or others. He is quoted as saying, "I don't want them to forget Ruth. I just want them to remember me." And he is clear that he cannot waste precious energy letting the hatred of others deflect him from his goal. We can talk about how we can show assertiveness in tense situations, about ways to stay focused on our goals.

We can also talk about how we can support someone's efforts to be assertive. In *Teammates*, Pee Wee Reese refuses to sign a petition saying that the other players won't play if Robinson is hired. The petition dies. Later, in a dramatic moment when angry fans are screaming racial epithets at Robinson, Reese walks from his position over to Robinson and puts his arm around his shoulder in a show of public support. In this book, although Aaron presumably met with racism within the team, the focus is on the fans. And many fans rallied around him. We can ask how we can take assertive action to support others when we see them struggling.

Just sticking with the sport of baseball, we can look at other people who have overcome prejudice with graceful courage, such as Hank Greenberg, who faced anti-Semitism when he played in the major league, and the young girls who became the first to play in the formerly all-male Little League.

Unit 4: Assertiveness   Grade 3

Book Talk

READ ALOUD

Previewing the book

Show the cover of the book. Ask students what they know about Hank Aaron. What do they think the subtitle means? Give some historical background about the Great Depression and segregation in the entire country. Not only were sports teams segregated, so were the Armed Forces, as well as schools, hotels, and restaurants in the South. Jackie Robinson could not stay in the same hotels with his teammates. This book doesn't say so, but until desegregation at least in the South, neither could Hank Aaron.

Reading and responding to the book

Read the story.

You may wish to pause at certain points to explain some things (p. 8, use of the word "colored," asking who knows who Jackie Robinson is, the fact that the Dodgers were once in Brooklyn; p. 21, the picture in the background is of Babe Ruth).

After you read the story, ask the students to pair up and talk about the book. What interests them? What questions do they have? Ask what was important to them about this story. Encourage the students to respond to each other by asking questions such as, "Do the rest of you agree or disagree with _____?" If others want to respond to a comment from one student, suggest that they restate in their own words what the student has said, then give their opinion and their reasons.

Deepening students' understanding of the book

Ask students to recap the book. Ask how a biography is different from a fictional story. Note that often in children's literature a writer will create a fictional story that fits with the known facts about a person's life. In this case, the author seems to have stuck to known facts. He has kept the focus completely on Aaron's achievement of his goals. Our focus here is on Aaron's strength of character and assertiveness. Introduce the concept of assertiveness, of being strong but not mean. We want students to look for examples of Hank's assertiveness throughout the book.

On p. 10, Hank is afraid to ask his mother for permission to play with the Black Bears. What does he think her objections are? (Many students may not know how strong the Christian influence regarding Sunday as a day of rest was in this country up until the last twenty or thirty years. There were laws against buying and selling on the Sabbath. Many Christians refused to violate the Sabbath by working or even engaging in recreation, such as going to the movies on Sunday.) How does the win-win solution work for both Hank and his mother?

On p. 12, when Estella Aaron tells Hank to "be strong," what do you think she is thinking of? What strength will it take for him to stay focused on his goal of getting in to the major leagues?

On p. 20, Hank decided to "fight the best way he could." Why is it the "best" way? What other options did he have? How might the story have been different if he had responded differently?

On p. 30, Hank thanks God for "pulling him through." What do students think he is particularly thankful for? Is it just for his talent and for beating Babe Ruth's record, or could it be for the strength to endure the hatred and triumph over it, or for his parents still being alive to see his achievement? What do we know about Estella Aaron's faith? Do we think she taught Hank to have faith in God?

Connecting the book to students' lives

Discussion: Have the students ever had a goal that they focused on? What strategies helped them obtain it? What do they think Hank had to do to achieve his goal? (Play a lot of ball, keep going to school, not believe white people's perception of black ballplayers' talents?)

What do the students think now about the book's subtitle "Brave in Every Way"? Ask students for ideas of how Hank was brave, then list them on the board (playing with adults, asking his mother when he knew she wouldn't approve of playing on Sunday, walking out on the field after he received death threats, and so on).

Ask students for examples of times they have been brave or have seen people be brave.

Writing: Write about a time when you were brave, or a time when you accomplished something good that you wanted to do, or a time when you saw something that was unfair.

Think of something you are passionate about doing. Imagine that there is now a law that people who have your color of hair cannot do this thing. Write a letter to the editor of the paper telling what you think of this law.

Draw a picture of yourself using a skill that you have.

ROLE-PLAY

Ask for volunteers to act out Hank and his father talking about Hank's dream of playing in the major leagues. What advice will his father give him? Ask for volunteers to play Hank and his mother when Hank asks if he can play with the Black Bears. How does he persuade her?

Unit 4: Assertiveness   Grade 3

Applied Learning

Introductory Note to the Teacher

Children meet situations every day in which they must decide how to balance their own interests in relation to the interests of other people:

- You want to be alone, but a friend wants to be with you. What do you do?

- A classmate teases you or calls you a name. How do you respond?

- You're walking along a busy city street with your mom and decide you want an ice cream cone. You know your mom won't be enthusiastic about the idea. How do you ask?

- Your family is having a conversation around the dinner table, and you have an opinion you'd like to state, but everyone is talking so fast. How do you get people to listen to what <u>you</u> have to say?

- An older kid says you have to give him the cake from your lunch or he'll beat you up. Two close friends ask you to join them in stealing money from another kid's backpack.

- Your younger brother keeps bothering you when you're trying to do your homework.

In these situations, children need to know that they have choices. They can go on the attack. They can stand up for their interests or convictions. Or they can give in, going along with the other person's request, even though they don't want to. Adults call these choices "aggression," "assertiveness," and "submission." With children, we speak of being mean, being strong, and giving in.

Although in this guide we're partial to assertiveness, there is no one right way to respond to the myriad of complex situations children (or adults) confront daily. Sometimes we'll agree to "give in" and let a friend join us even if we really want to be alone. We may see that the friend is feeling blue and needs some companionship; or perhaps the friend has a compelling reason for spending time with us now—she's going away or has something important to tell us. Sometimes we may need to be very firm to get our point across to someone who just "isn't getting it," and that person may experience us as mean.

Our aim is that children learn to think flexibly in order to come up with the approach that fits the situation and develop skills to carry it out. This means showing youngsters that they have a range of choices in any given situation and expanding their repertoire of ways to be strong. Too often children (and adults) in our society fall into the habit of being aggressive or submissive rather than taking the path that is usually most effective in the long run: assertiveness.

Like active listening, assertiveness is a stance toward life, a way of being in the world. Like active listening, assertiveness also involves a set of skills we can practice and improve. With young children (grades K-2) we focus on the most basic skills of assertiveness: saying no; and making a strong, clear, confident statement of what you want. With older children, we introduce additional strategies, such as "I-messages."

In Book Talk, we've introduced some of these ideas about assertiveness as they relate to the story. Here in the Applied Learning Section, we give children a chance to deepen their thinking and develop their skills.

Lesson 1

Objectives

Students will
- observe a role-play in which two friends are having a conflict
- apply the Plan 1-2-3 technique introduced in Unit 2
- describe the problem and how the characters are feeling
- identify choices the characters have in the situation

Materials Needed

- agenda on chart paper or the chalkboard

Gathering: A Strong Wind Blows

You and the children are sitting in chairs in a circle. Stand up, remove your chair from the circle and put it aside, and then go to the center of the circle. Thus, there's one less chair than the number of participants. Explain that when you say, A Strong Wind Blows on _____, you want everyone mentioned to change seats. You'll be trying to get a seat too. The person who ends up without a seat is "it" and will be the one to make the strong wind blow next. They are not to leave their seat until you're done saying whom the strong wind blows on. You can start by using children's names; for example, A strong wind blows on Jose, Yvette, Chavonne, and Amy. But it's usually more fun to have the strong wind blow on whole categories of children; for example: a strong wind blows on everyone who is wearing sneakers; a strong wind blows on everyone who had cereal for breakfast this morning. And so on.

Check agenda

Go over the objectives and the agenda.

Choices

Role-plays are useful for working on assertiveness with students in Grades 3-5. The role-play below picks up on the theme of being different as well as on the challenge of standing up to peer pressure. If it doesn't seem appropriate for your class, please create another tailored to your class's needs or use one of the many other possible role-plays described below (see "Other Situations" on page 70).

Here's the situation. Jennie is different from the other kids in the class in several ways: she always wears dresses (rather than the dungarees and t-shirts the other kids wear); the dresses often seem out of style and a bit big on her; she's shy; and whether in the classroom,

Unit 4: Assertiveness — Grade 3

the lunchroom or the school yard, she always carries a notebook around with her for her favorite activity, writing.

Victoria is the most popular girl in the class, a leader. She decides she wants to have some fun by getting several other girls to join her in a plan to get Jennie's notebook away from her and hide it.

Victoria approaches Latoya, one of several girls in the class who like to hang out with her, and tells her of the plan. "The only time she isn't holding that stupid notebook is when she works at the computer," says Victoria. "Watch her closely and when you get your chance, take the notebook and give it to me. I'll find a good place for it."

Latoya admires Victoria and enjoys being her friend. Being friends with Victoria gives her status in the class. However, she doesn't like this idea. First, she's pretty sure that if she takes part in the scheme, she'll get in trouble. But she also has nothing against Jennie. Sure, she's a little strange, but Jennie has always been nice to her; in fact, Jennie gave her half of her sandwich when she'd forgotten her lunch one day.

So Latoya doesn't want to take part in Victoria's plan. In fact, she doesn't want Victoria to do anything to hurt Jennie. But it's also important for her to remain Victoria's friend. And she doesn't want the other kids in the class to look down on her, as they do Jennie.

Ask for three volunteers: one to play Victoria, one to play Latoya, and one to be the narrator (who will fill in necessary background). Brief your actors on their roles. Make name tags for them with the names they will have in the role-play. Use the names suggested above only if they are the names of no children in your class.

A good ritual for beginning role-plays is to lead the class saying in unison, "Lights, camera, action!"

Run the skit.

Use Plan 1-2-3, "Stop, Breathe, Think" (Unit 2, Lesson 4, page 31) to freeze the action while Victoria is still trying to convince Latoya to help her carry out her plan.

Ask, what is happening? Encourage the students to describe what is going on as objectively as possible. Then ask, how do you think the characters are feeling?

Ask, what are Latoya's choices? What are the different ways she might deal with the situation?

Elicit the student's ideas and chart them. Push them to come up with a wide range of possibilities.

Discuss: What do you think is the right thing for Latoya to do in this situation? Why? Do you think that will be easy or hard for her? What would you do? Why?

Evaluation

What was your favorite activity in this lesson?

Closing: Applause

Lead the students in a round of applause.

Lesson 2

Objectives

Students will
- learn the words "strong," "mean," and "giving in" to describe the choices they have in conflict situations;
- apply those ideas to clarify the choices faced by characters in a role-play;
- practice predicting the results or consequences of certain choices.

Materials Needed

- agenda on chart paper or the chalkboard

Gathering: Freeze

Play a piece of music and ask students to move around the room in any way they choose, while respecting others' personal space. Tell the students that when the music stops, they should "freeze" as if they are a statue. They can move only when the music starts again. While "frozen," they can take a moment to notice each other's statues. Repeat several times, varying the amount of time that you let the music play. This develops listening skills and the ability to physically self-monitor and self-regulate.

Go over the objectives and the agenda.

Strong, Mean, and Giving In

Introduce the words "strong," "mean," and "giving in." The children will probably have a good idea of the usual meanings of these words. Elicit their understandings. Then summarize the discussion by putting forth the following definitions:

- Strong = being nice and respecting the other person while standing up firmly for yourself (your rights, your interests);
- Mean = doing something to hurt another person (their body or their feelings) or using force or threats to make somebody do something they don't want to do;
- Giving in = going along with what someone wants you to do even though you'd rather do something else.

Unit 4: Assertiveness　　　　　　　　　　　　　　　　　　　　　　　　　　　　Grade 3

For each of the three definitions, elicit examples from the children. (Depending on the age and maturity of your students, you may also want to introduce them to the "adult" words: assertive, aggressive, and submissive.)

Now apply those categories of response to the choices Latoya had in her interaction with Victoria. Which were "giving in"? Which were "strong"? Were any "mean"?

Consequences

Refer to the role-play with Victoria and Latoya. Ask the children to recall the situation. Say that one way to make a good choice is to think ahead about what is likely to happen as a result of your choice.

Select student volunteers to replay the skit as before, except this time they will act out one of the ideas the class proposed as choices for Latoya. Confer with the student playing Latoya and ask her to decide which course of action she'll have Latoya follow. It can be any of the choices; it doesn't have to be the one the student thinks is best.

Run the skit: "Lights, camera, action!"

Freeze the action after the two characters have had some dialogue back and forth. Ask the students to describe what has happened in the role-play. What choice did the character Latoya make? How has Victoria responded? What do they think will happen next?

Have student actors act out several of Latoya's choices and discuss as above. The aim is not to arrive at a definitive answer about what will happen in any given situation, but to show the children that it's possible—and important—to anticipate consequences.

Evaluation

What's one thing you want to remember from our lesson today?

Closing: Doing Something I Enjoyed

In pairs, students describe to each other a time when they did something well and enjoyed doing it. Ask for a few volunteers to share with the group.

Lesson 3

Objective

Students will learn "I-messages" as one technique for assertive or "strong" behavior.

Materials Needed

- agenda on chart paper or the chalkboard
- copies of I-Message form (page 81)

Gathering: Freeze 2

Repeat the "freeze" activity from Unit 4, Lesson 2. This time, when you stop the music, call out either "strong," "mean," or "giving in." Students must make a statue that expresses their understanding of these terms.

After a few minutes, ask students to say what they noticed about the statues for each term. How were they different? How did each posture feel?

Check agenda

Go over the objectives and agenda

I-Messages

So far we've been helping students with two kinds of assertiveness skills: saying no; and stating clearly and confidently what you want or what you believe to be right. Here we introduce a strategy that is sometimes useful in dealing with problems that come up with friends and family, that is, people who are likely to care about our feelings.

Begin by writing "I-message" on the board. Explain that today the students will learn what an I-message is and how to construct one.

An I-message is a way to be strong without being mean when you are angry or upset or disappointed (or whatever) with something another person has done. The formula for an I-message is as follows:

> I feel _____
> (state your feeling)
>
> when you _____
> (describe the specific behavior)
>
> because _____
> (state the effect the behavior has on you)

The "I-message" is distinguished from a "You-message." In a "You-message," you attack the other person, make judgments about him, and sometimes even call him names.

For example, say your younger brother borrows your bat and leaves it at a friend's house. A "You-message" would be: "You little jerk. How could you be so stupid! Now I don't have my bat when I need it!"

In this situation, what would an "I-message" be? Elicit possible "I-messages" from the students (for example: I feel frustrated when you borrow my bat and leave it at your friend's house, because I need it today and it's not here).

Discuss: What are your comments about these two ways of communicating feelings? Can you see using an I-message the next time you feel like calling somebody a name? Why? Why not?

Have students work in pairs to complete the worksheet on I-messages (page 73). You can use the "Assertiveness line" (page 69) and "Strong Message Machine" ("Additional Activities," page 70) to give them more practice.

Draining**

Invite students to stand up and think of a situation in which they felt angry or fearful. Ask them to tense their muscles and hold tightly for a few seconds. Then tell them to relax and feel the emotion draining out of them into a puddle at their feet. Then, have them step aside, leaving the feeling behind.

Ask students what this was like. When could you use this? They may make connections to the idea that using "strong" messages and I-messages is easier when we have recognized and released some of our anger or fear. They may also note that Hank Aaron had to find ways to manage his strong emotions in order to stay focused on his goal.

** Adapted from *Creative Conflict Resolution* by William Kreidler, p. 120.

Evaluation and Closing: Connections

Set a timer for three minutes. Explain that this is a time to pause and think back over today's lesson or anything else that has happened today that's on your mind. Nobody has to say anything, but if anybody wants to say something to the group, they can raise their hand, you'll give them the Hugg-A-Planet or listening stick, and they can talk. People can share something they learned, something they're thinking about, a feeling they're having, whatever. Tell them to keep their comments brief so that others can talk. When the time runs out, "Connections" is over.

Lesson 4

Objectives

Students will
- practice "strong" (assertive) behavior in role-plays;
- continue to deepen their understanding of "strong," "mean," and "giving in" by discussing which of the categories applies to specific examples.

Materials Needed

- agenda on chart paper or chalkboard

Gathering: Louder/Softer

Repeat the "Louder/Softer" activity from Unit 3, Lesson 4, page 58.

Discuss with the class: What volume might you use when communicating with an I-Message? Why? There is no right or wrong answer to this question, as each situation might call for a different volume. Encourage students to think about how the volume in which an I-statement is communicated might affect how it is received.

Check agenda

Go over the objectives and the agenda.

Assertiveness Line

Role-plays in front of the class are useful for introducing ideas (such as, choice, consequences, and assertiveness). But only a few students are actively participating while most of the class observes. Other kinds of activities are necessary to give the students practice.

In an "assertiveness line," the students form two lines with students in Line A facing students in Line B so that each student has a partner.

You can say, "All the students in this line are Student A and all the students in this line are Student B. Student A was using a marker. S/he put it down for a minute to ask the teacher a question. Student B took the marker and is now using it. Student A wants the marker back. Does everybody understand the situation? Okay. When I say 'Go,' begin acting out the situation. When I say 'Freeze,' stop immediately and get quiet. No touching the other person." (You may want to practice the freeze command with the students several times to show them that you expect them to stop immediately and be completely quiet.)

Say "Go!" Let the action run for a minute or so. Stop the action. Ask, what happened in your pairs? How did Child A try to get the marker back? What did Child B do? As volunteers share what happened in their pair, ask, what kind of response was that? Strong? Mean? Giving in? After hearing from several pairs, say that when you say Go, you want them to do the skit again. This time you want Child A in all of the pairs to try a strong response.

Continue with other situations. Make up ones relevant to your class or use the suggestions included in this unit under "Additional Activities." If a second scenario is used, ask the students to use Plan 1-2-3, "Stop, Breathe, Think" (Unit 2, Lesson 4, page 31and then continue their role-play. Have students compare the first and second scenarios. Did using the "Stop, Breathe, Think" approach change how the role-play went?

Evaluation

Was it easy or hard to think of "strong" things to do in your assertiveness line? Can you see yourself acting that way in real life? Why? Why not?

Unit 4: Assertiveness   Grade 3

Closing: Pass the Sound

Play "Pass the Sound," as in Unit 1, page 10. Begin by making a sound. "Pass" the sound to a student. Ask the student to imitate the sound you are making and then change it into another sound. S/he passes it to another person who repeats the new sound and changes it again. Continue around the group.

Additional Activities

Other Situations

Invent other skits that present situations students encounter daily. Choose situations that your particular class is confronting and struggling with. Use the skits to deepen their awareness of choices and consequences and to increase their repertoire of "strong" responses. Here's a list of the kinds of situations in which students may find "strong" or assertive behavior helpful:

- expressing needs or desires clearly and firmly without whining;
- dealing with teasing;
- dealing with bullying;
- dealing with peer pressure;
- dealing with problems with friends (hurt feelings, misunderstandings, broken promises, etc.)
- dealing with things that don't seem fair.

Here are some possible scenarios for skits:

- Yvonne is teasing Jessica, saying she's fat or she talks funny or her hair is too short or whatever. [You supply the specific pretext for the teasing based on the kinds of things that come up in your class. But avoid choosing a scenario that directly calls attention to a specific instance of teasing and therefore might add to the hurt of the child who was teased.] Ask the class to imagine themselves as a third person seeing this. Yvonne is a leader in the class. Jessica is not popular but she's always been nice to you. You as a third party want to stop the teasing. What can you do?

- The same skit as above (between Yvonne and Jessica), but this time, no one else is around. What can Jessica do?

- John approaches his best friend Sean and offers him a candy bar. "Where did you get it?" Sean asks. "From Joan's backpack," whispers John. "No one saw me take it." Sean is afraid of getting in trouble if he takes the stolen candy. He doesn't want to do it. What does he say to John?

- Betty and Naomi are good friends. They agree that tomorrow they'll dress exactly the same—all in black. They agree that if for some reason one person can't do this, then that person will be sure to call the other to let her know. Betty comes to school all dressed in black, but Naomi comes in blue dungarees and a red shirt. Betty is furious. What does she do?

Strong Message Machine

This is another activity that gives children the opportunity for practice. Have them form two lines facing each other as for the Assertiveness Line above. But this time, they are a "Strong Message Machine." Present a situation. Two kids are teasing another child because they say he talks funny. "You can't talk!" They chant. "You can't talk!" The child has just come to New York City from another country. He's just learning English. You want the kids to stop teasing him. What do you do?

Ask the children to talk with their partners (that is, the child facing them in the line) and think of a strong message to give the teasers to make them stop. Give them a minute to come up with something.

Then the teacher walks between the two lines. She stops at a child and pretends to "turn the child on" (by pressing an imaginary button or turning a knob). That child says a strong message. The teacher says "Thank you," and then walks further down between the lines, stopping to turn another child on and hear his or her strong message. And so on.

After you're done with the machine, discuss: What were your favorite "strong" messages? Why did you like them?

Make time for silence

During this time the lights are off. No writing, drawing, reading, no gadgets. Just sitting. Encourage students to put their hands on their knees. Students can close their eyes if they want. You can tell them that they can let their minds use the silence as they wish. Or you can suggest ways they might use the silence. For example,

- Practice abdominal breathing (introduced in Unit 2)
- Simply pay attention to your breathing
- Pay attention to sounds you hearIn your mind, take yourself to a peaceful place
- Recall a time you had fun
- Recall something you like to do

After the time of silence, ask for a couple of volunteers to share where their minds went during the time. Make time for silence every day, preferably at the same time, such as after lunch or recess or the first and last actions of the day.

By giving students the opportunity to experience time for silence on a daily basis, you'll be instilling a habit that will serve them well for the rest of their lives.

Consider having your students keep a 4Rs journal

Writing (drawing for younger students) is an excellent way to reinforce and consolidate learning. A journal enables students to put all of their Book Talk writing in one place. You can also give them a few minutes after each 4Rs lesson to jot down a few thoughts about what they're taking away or how they're planning to use what they've just learned. If a student tries a new skill, s/he might want to write about what happened. Did it bring a positive result? If a student is stuck in a conflict with someone, s/he might want to do some writing to sort it out and imagine some solutions. You can give them standard journals and encourage them to decorate them.

By having students keep journals, you will be introducing them to a habit or practice that can serve them well the rest of their lives.

Related Books

The Bat Boy and his Violin by Gavin Curtis

Crow Boy by Taro Yashima

Dark Day, Light Night by Jan Carr, illustrated by James Ransome

The Gift-Giver by Joyce Hansen

I'm In Charge of Celebrations by Byrd Baylor, illustrated by Peter Parnall

Teammates by Peter Golenbock, illustrated by Paul Bacon

Handout 1 • Unit 4

Design an I-Message
for each of the following situations:

1. You lent your new bike to a friend. When s/he returns it, it has a flat tire.

   I feel _____

   when you _____

   because _____

2. You're standing in the water fountain line. All of a sudden, two students push right in front of you.

   I feel _____

   when you _____

   because _____

3. When you walk past Willie at recess, he calls you a name under his breath.

   I feel _____

   when you _____

   because _____

4. When you get home from school, you go to the kitchen to get a piece of pie. It turns out that your sister just ate the last two pieces.

   I feel _____

   when you _____

   because _____

Blank by design.

3

Unit 5 Theme

Solving Problems Collaboratively

Unit 5 Book Selection

Old Henry by Joan W. Blos
Mulberry Books, 1990

Activities

- Reviewing the definition of "conflict"
- Win-Win Solutions
- Creative Conflict Solving
- Problem Solving: ABCDE approach
- Balancing
- Additional Activities

Introduction

Conflict. The word can make our stomachs tense or send adrenaline rushing through our bodies. Most people have a flight or fight reaction to conflict, and most people don't think of conflict as a constructive force. In this unit we will look at conflict both as a process to be managed or resolved without flight or a violent fight and as a force that in some cases can deepen our self-knowledge and lead to closeness and personal growth. We will look at varieties of conflicts, especially those in school, and varieties of responses. We will sharpen our ability to deal well with conflict by applying skills from previous units and practicing some new skills, such as win-win negotiation. Although it is not possible for every conflict to be solved to the satisfaction of all parties, our emphasis will be on learning to reach win-win solutions.

Conflict is a natural part of life. We encounter conflict every day. Some conflicts are inevitable (clashes over opposing needs, goals, or values), and some are unnecessary or avoidable (results of misunderstandings, ignorance, prejudice, poor organizational structure, poor communication, etc.). Conflicts bring up feelings, which is perfectly natural. Although we often think that conflict must lead to violence, it doesn't have to, especially if we have skills in conflict resolution.

Robert Bolton, in *People Skills*, identifies three kinds of conflicts: conflicts of emotion, of values, and of need. Active listening is key in dealing with conflicts of emotion. Value conflicts can seldom be resolved, but conflict resolution skills can help the parties understand each other better and show greater tolerance. Conflicts of need can often be resolved through the methods covered in this unit: negotiation, mediation, and problem solving. Ironically, the avoidable conflicts rooted in misunderstanding and prejudice may be less amenable to these methods and may best be dealt with through assertiveness.

> **Negotiation** is a process by which two or more parties talk together in order to arrive at an agreement. We all negotiate every day.
>
> ---
>
> **Mediation** is a process in which a neutral facilitator helps parties to a dispute talk out their differences. The decision-making power stays in the hands of the disputants.
>
> ---
>
> **Arbitration** is a process in which disputants present their points of view to a judge or arbitrator, who hands down a decision.

In this unit

	Ideas	Skills
Literacy	<ul><li>Stories have characters</li><li>Sometimes we can use stories to understand our own lives</li><li>Words and pictures together can tell a story</li><li>Stories often show conflicts</li></ul>	<ul><li>Summarizing the action</li><li>Predicting</li><li>Identifying the main idea</li><li>Asking questions</li><li>Expressing ideas clearly</li><li>Providing evidence to back up one's assertions</li></ul>
Social and Emotional Learning	<ul><li>A conflict is a disagreement, an argument, or a fight</li><li>Conflict is a natural part of life</li><li>Conflict can lead to violence but it doesn't have to, especially if you have skills in conflict resolution</li><li>We can find solutions to many conflicts</li><li>Conflicts can have solutions where everyone is happy</li></ul>	<ul><li>Finding win-win solutions to conflicts</li><li>Paying attention to what is going on in a conflict</li><li>Identifying feelings in a conflict</li><li>Generating solutions to conflicts</li><li>Using the ABCDE problem solving process to solve problems.</li></ul>

Unit 5: Problem Solving Grade 3

Old Henry, by Joan W. Blos, illustrated by Stephen Gammell.
Mulberry Books, imprint of William Morrow and Company, Inc., 1990.

SUMMARY

"The story begins when a stranger appears/and moves into a house that was vacant for years." The stranger is Old Henry, the house is "drafty, dark, and gray," but it suits "him from inside out." He loves all its spaces, which would house all his things. The neighbors are relieved to see someone move in. They tell each other he will soon "fix things up a bit." But he "did not think of it." Soon, people are whispering, " 'That place is a disgrace.'" But he doesn't notice "(or else didn't care)."

The muttering grows, the neighbors form a committee. They ask him to improve the looks of the property. He listens politely and goes "back to his book." The committee enlists the power of the state (in this case, the town), which fines him for violations, threatens jail, sends long letters. Nothing works. The committee goes to the mayor, who suggests "being nice." The committee is aghast, but the mayor urges them to "try it twice." Two women bake him a pie, which he refuses. Three men offer to shovel his snow, and he turns them down. But he's gotten the message: "I never will/ live like the rest of them, neat and the same./I am sorry I came." He packs up and leaves a sign on the door saying, "Gone to Dakota."

He's gone, but the neighbors are not necessarily happy. His garden blooms, his apples need to be picked, the snow piles up again. They ask themselves if he will come back. "The house looks so empty, so dark in the night/And having him gone doesn't make us more right." Belatedly they realize that "we don't have to make such a terrible fuss/because everyone isn't exactly like us." Meanwhile, Henry is camped out on the Dakota plains, missing the neighbors "who'd brought him the pies./ In spite of their nagging, he really did care/for them and their street. So he wrote the mayor." If he mends the gate and shovels the snow, "would they not scold my birds?/ Could I let my grass grow?"

We don't know the answer, but we can hope for the best.

COMMENT

In an earlier grade, students read *The Big Orange Splot*, in which the neighborhood dissident persuades the rest of the neighborhood to express their individuality. In this story, the differences are more intractable. The neighborhood residents find nothing commendable in the laissez-faire behavior of Old Henry. They value neatness and conformity. He values solitude and individuality. The committee tries the usual tactics, starting with discussion, then moving to intimidation. The mayor counsels niceness, which at first doesn't seem to work. No one suggests listening to each other. There is no evidence that either side actually hears the other. However, the interactions, unsatisfactory as they are, keep the lines of communication open. If the neighbors had used only legal sanction, Henry would not have been likely to suggest a solution.

We can look at the different characters and examine why they act as they do. We can see various problem-solving strategies in play and brainstorm others. We can explore the feelings that each participant might have. We can talk about our own conflicts with the norms of the group. We can ask what our classroom community can tolerate and what it can't. We can enjoy the lyrical watercolors and the lilting rhymes.

This is the second narrative poem we've read that illustrates a conflict-resolution theme. (The first was *The Pain and the Great One*.) We can contrast and compare the poems, we can note the rhythm, the repetition of "That Henry" every few pages.

Book Talk

READ ALOUD

Previewing the book

Look at the cover and ask the students what they think the book will be about. Show the title page. What thoughts do the students have about what they see? Explain that this story is a poem in rhyme. The previous two books we have looked at have been prose poems.

Reading and responding to the book

Read the story. You might pause at some points to ask what the students think will happen next, for instance, p. 19, after the second attempt at "niceness" from the neighbors or p. 27, as the neighbors are missing Henry.

Deepening students' understanding of the book

After you read the story, ask the students to pair up and talk about the book. What interests them? What questions do they have?

In the general discussion, draw out as many ideas as possible about the themes of the book. Our emphasis in this unit is on problem solving. Henry's independence and unconcern for community standards has led to conflict with the neighbors (or, we could say that their over-concern for neat lawns and well-kept houses has led the neighbors into conflict with him, since there is no hint that he is causing a health hazard). Both sides want to continue living in the neighborhood.

Read the book again and say that this time we are going to look for the conflicts (including the first signs, such as when we watch Henry move in and hear the neighbors assure each other that he'll fix up the place), the feelings of the characters, and how they change as a result of the conflict. Make a T-chart and write Henry in one column and Neighbors in another. What do we know about Henry from the description of his belongings and activities (p. 8, 12); what can we guess about the neighbors from looking at them and their houses (pp. 6,9)? Put stars next to the items that we think are most important to Henry and to the neighbors. How do these values set the stage for a conflict? What is the big conflict here? Why?

Knowing what we know about these characters, can we brainstorm some different courses of action for them, keeping in mind what is most important to them? Remind the class that brainstorming means throwing out ideas but not discussing them. Just list the ideas.

Make a Venn diagram of feelings that both parties have before Henry leaves. Write how you think the neighbors are feeling in one color and how Henry is feeling in another. Are some of the feelings the same?

Draw a time line: Henry leaves; Henry is gone for almost a year; Henry wants to come back. What feelings do Henry and the neighbors have at each point? We may have to guess a little, but should be able to back up each assertion. What caused people to change their minds and feel differently?

What did each party learn from the conflict?

Connecting the book to students' lives

Discussion: Has anyone ever had a conflict with someone about being messy (either the other person thought you were too messy or vice versa)? Pair up with someone and talk about that conflict.

Has anyone ever known anyone who was considered "different"? Did their being different lead to conflicts? Point out that being different doesn't always lead to conflicts, but sometimes does if there are conflicts of values. Invite students to take a moment of silence to think about these questions and to take a deep breath before and after speaking. Silence and deep breathing encourage thoughtful focus on the topic. Talk with a partner about situations you have seen and then share with the group.

Review the rules of the classroom. How would Henry fit into your classroom? What do you think would happen if he came into the class as a child? What would the class and the teacher be happy about and what might they not be happy about (he's a good reader, good cook, has a pet parrot, minds his own business, doesn't clean up, etc.). Do the same for the neighbors.

Have you ever wanted to ignore the rules of a group (for instance, changing the rules of a game you are playing)? Talk about that with a partner.

Writing: Write a dialogue or play in which two things, animals, or people have a conflict and then try many ways to solve it. What is the solution they finally agree to?

Look at the timeline of the story. Ask students to be either Henry, the parrot, a neighbor, the mayor, or any other character in the story and write a diary entry for the beginning of the story when Henry first arrives, during the time that he is gone, and when he is thinking about coming back. What are you thinking and feeling at each time?

Ask students to pretend that they are newspaper reporters who have heard about what is happening. Write a story for the paper about the conflict in this town.

ROLE-PLAY

Break into pairs and have one person be the mayor and another a neighbor who is complaining about Henry. The mayor should defend Henry as much as s/he can.

A more ambitious role-play is to organize a town meeting in which the neighbors talk about what to do about Henry. There could be different roles, i.e., the mayor, children who like the birds, neighbors who hate the unmowed grass, etc. The group could look at the list of ideas that the class brainstormed earlier in order to think of possible actions.

Applied Learning

Lesson 1

Objectives

Students will
- be able to define the word conflict, give examples of conflicts, and distinguish conflict from violence;
- learn that conflicts can have different outcomes (win-win, win-lose, and lose-lose) and practice categorizing conflicts accordingly;
- generate ideas for win-win solutions for a conflict.

Materials Needed

- agenda on chart paper or the white board
- chart of "Ways Conflicts Can Turn Out" on chart paper or the white board (page 83)
- "There Is Always Something You Can Do" song sheet (page 98)

Gathering: Count to Five

In this game the class tries to count to five by people in the class calling out numbers. Sound easy? There's a catch. If two people call out a number at the same time, the class has to start over. Introduce the game by explaining the rules:

- Anyone can call out a number, starting with one.
- The count has to go in order (that is, one, two, three, four, five).
- If two people say the same number at the same time, the class has to start over.
- The object of the game is to get to five before the timer goes off.

The teacher will serve as the judge of whether two people called a number at the same time. Set a timer for three minutes and begin.

Discuss: How was this game? What made it hard? What strategies did you come up with to overcome the challenge? (Some that may be discussed include listening, paying close attention, being aware of or "tuning in" to others, observing, etc. Emphasize that these are all important skills for active listening and problem solving.)

If the group doesn't succeed in getting to five, tell them they can try it again another day. If the group quickly masters the task, you can have them try to reach higher and higher numbers.

Check agenda

Go over the objectives and the agenda.

Reviewing the definition of "conflict"

Your students have encountered the concept of conflict in Unit 3 on Listening (*The Pain and the Great One*). They discussed the meaning of the word and drew pictures of conflict situations. They have discussed conflict again in Book Talk for this unit in connection with the conflict between Old Henry and his neighbors. Since conflict is central to this lesson and the activities that follow, review the working definition of conflict as "an argument, a disagreement, or a fight."

To deepen students' understanding of the concept, you may want to distinguish it from violence. Ask the children if they know what violence is. From a brief discussion, develop a working definition of violence as "people hurting other people on purpose." Make the point that sometimes a conflict can lead to violence but it doesn't have to. Through 4Rs lessons, we're learning peaceful ways to solve conflicts so that they don't lead to violence.

Win-Win Solutions

With another adult or a student volunteer, role-play the following conflict:

Adrienne, Malkia and several of their friends have been working hard on a play, which they plan to present to the class. They have created the characters and written a script. The main character is a young woman named Sheeba who uses her skill in the martial arts to stop evil people from stealing people's pets.

Everything is going along fine until one day an argument breaks out between Adrienne and Malkia over who gets to play Sheeba.

> "I've decided I'd like to play Sheeba!" says Adrienne.
>
> "That's not fair," protests Malkia. "We agreed from the beginning that I would be Sheeba."
>
> "I know but I've changed my mind," replies Adrienne. "I'd really like to play Sheeba. Anyway, I've written most of her lines."
>
> "But I've made her costume with my mother," says Malkia. "I want to be Sheeba!"

"You don't even know martial arts," says Adrienne. "It'll be hard for you to learn Sheeba's moves. I'm a green belt in Taekwondo."

Freeze the action using Plan 1-2-3, "Stop, Breathe, Think" (Unit 2, Lesson 5, page 35) and discuss: What is happening? How are the characters feeling? What do they want? Elicit that the two characters are having a conflict because they both want to play Sheeba.

Then ask, What could happen next? Elicit the students' thinking about possible outcomes. [Malkia could let Adrienne have the role. Adrienne could let Malkia have the role. They could get into a fight and get so angry at each other that they cancel the play. Or the teacher might intervene and make the decision for them.]

If the students don't come up with it a win-win solution on their own, ask, How might the two girls solve this conflict so that both of them could get what they want? [They might share the role—for example, one is Sheeba for half of the play, and the other is Sheeba for the other half; or if they perform the play more than once, they could take turns playing Sheeba. They might agree to write another episode of Sheeba's story so that the one who doesn't play Sheeba this time could play her next time. They could create another strong female character that serves as Sheeba's partner. And so on.]

Now role-play the various outcomes the students have come up with. Begin with an outcome in which Adrienne and Malkia fight and the play is ruined. Ask, Did the characters get what they wanted? How are they feeling? Explain that because the characters didn't get what they wanted and are both feeling sad and disappointed, we call this a lose-lose solution. Then go on to dramatize and name a win-lose solution and a win-win solution. After each dramatization, be sure to ask how the characters are feeling.

Having introduced the concepts of win-win, win-lose, and lose-lose solutions through the role-plays, you can reinforce them with this chart:

Ways Conflicts Can Turn Out

	Adrienne gets what she wants	Adrienne doesn't get what she wants
Malkia gets what she wants	Win-Win	Win-Lose
Malkia doesn't get what she wants	Lose-Win	Lose-Lose

Ask the students to think of recent conflicts they've seen or been involved in. After a student has described a conflict, ask how it turned out. After a student shares a conflict and its outcome, ask the class, What kind of solution was that? Win-Win? Win-Lose? Lose-Lose? Discuss.

Ask, What kind of outcome do you think is best? Win-Win? Win-Lose? Lose-Lose? Why? Why not?

As conflicts arise in the classroom or you encounter conflicts in children's literature, you will have many opportunities to reinforce your students' understanding of the kinds of outcomes conflicts can have. You might begin by applying these concepts of win-win, win-lose, lose-lose to the conflicts in *Old Henry*.

Closing: "There Is Always Something You Can Do"

Teach the first verse of the song "There Is Always Something You Can Do." See the song sheet on page 98.

Lesson 2

Objective

Students will
- be keen observers, paying attention to what is happening in a conflict
- practice generating win-win solutions to a conflict

Materials Needed
- agenda on chart paper or the chalkboard

Gathering: "Stand Up"

Introduce the students to the "Stand Up" game. The teacher says, "Stand up if you're wearing anything that's blue." The students wearing blue stand up. The teacher says, "Okay. Thank you. Sit down," and then continues, "Stand up if you like pizza." And so on. Continue for several minutes if interest remains high. Invent "stand-ups" tailored to your class. Here are a few to get you started:

- Stand up if you have a pet at home
- Stand up if your birthday is this month
- Stand up if you're wearing sneakers
- Stand up if you like ice cream

When students are standing, you can ask one or two of them to share a bit more. For example, if students who have pets at home are standing, you can give them a chance to say what kind of pet they have and what its name is.

Check agenda

Go over the objectives and the agenda.

Creative Conflict Solving

In this activity, the teacher will be the facilitator, and two students will perform a skit. You will need to prepare the students ahead of time so that they're clear about their roles. Make nametags with the character's names for the students to play so that it's clear that they're playing a role. Here's the skit:

> Yvette grabs a pencil from Michael. "This pencil's mine!" says Yvette. "You thief! You stole it out of my desk! I've been looking for it all morning."
>
> Michael grabs the pencil back. "I did not steal it, liar! It's _my_ pencil. I brought it from home this morning."

Freeze the action, but ask the actors to stay in character. If it feels appropriate, remind the class that this is another time to use Plan 1-2-3, "Stop, Breathe, Think" (Unit 2, Lesson 4, page 31).

Ask the class, What is happening? Encourage the students to describe what's going on in a neutral, non-judgmental way. For example, a statement like "Michael stole Yvette's pencil and Yvette wants it back" contains an assumption that may or may not be true on the basis of the information provided in the skit. More objective statements would be: "There's one pencil and two students want it" or "Yvette has grabbed Michael's pencil, saying it's hers, but Michael has grabbed it back, saying it's his."

Ask, How are Yvette and Michael feeling? Encourage the students to make educated guesses about how the characters are feeling by reading their behavior, tone of voice, and body language, and then to ask the characters if their educated guesses are correct. Here they're practicing the skill of reflecting feelings, introduced in Unit 2.

Ask, Is there anything Yvette or Michael might have done differently? The students may say that Yvette could have asserted herself strongly about her pencil without calling Michael a thief and accusing him of stealing it. Michael could have protested his innocence and his ownership of the pencil without calling Yvette a liar.

Ask, If Yvette and Michael continue their grabbing and name-calling, how is this conflict likely to turn out? Elicit predictions from the students. For each likely outcome the students propose, ask if it is a win-win, win-lose, or lose-lose solution.

Ask, How might Yvette and Michael solve this problem so that it will work out well for both of them? The solution will have to address not only the issue of the pencil but hurt feelings resulting from the name-calling. Encourage the students to think of as many solutions as they can. Accept all ideas without judging them. When several ideas are on the table, propose them one at a time to the "Yvette" and "Michael" for their consideration. It's fine for Yvette and Michael to be feisty. They don't have to accept a solution the class offers if they don't think it's a good one.

After some back-and-forth with the class about their ideas for solutions, **ask one of the characters agree to act on one of the proposed ideas** for solving the conflict.

Continue the skit, with the characters coming to some kind of resolution.

Ask the class, What do you think of the solution the characters came up with? Did it solve the problem? How are Yvette and Michael feeling now? What kind of solution was it? Win-Win? Win-Lose? Lose-Lose? Was the solution realistic—could it happen in real life?

Ask, Do we ever have problems like this in our class? Elicit students' comments. With Yvette and Michael in mind, what shouldn't you do if you lose a pencil? What should you do?

> **Note to the teacher**
> By presenting a conflict and then guiding your students through the sequence of questions above, you are fostering a useful approach or "habit of mind" for dealing with conflict. To reinforce this way of thinking about conflict and enable your students to integrate it into their lives, use this activity frequently throughout the year, substituting other conflicts relevant to life in your classroom.

Closing: Quick, quick, slow

Ask students to stretch their arms above their heads, wiggle their fingers, and then drop their hands quickly into their laps. Repeat a second time. The third time, ask them to lower their hands slowly, taking perhaps 10-15 seconds to lower hands completely. Do this with students so that they follow your motions. Breathe! This activity encourages physical self-regulation and can be both energizing and calming.

Lesson 3

Objective
- Students will practice a basic problem-solving method by tackling an actual classroom problem.

Materials Needed
- agenda on chart paper or the chalkboard
- chart paper, markers, carpenter's tape
- chart paper with the A B C D E method of problem solving

Gathering: Alphabet Soup

Tell the students that you will shout out a letter from A to E and they will respond popcorn style with a word that starts with that letter. Encourage every student to participate.

Check agenda

Go over the objectives and agenda

Problem Solving

The ABCDE approach to problem-solving, conceived by William Kreidler, is a useful way to introduce students to creative problem-solving methods. Here we use the ABCDE approach to solve a class problem.

Choose a problem or issue that has been plaguing your class (for example, children keep losing their pencils, or squabbles break out daily at clean-up time, or a lot of tattling is going on). Or, if you wish, you can ask the class to brainstorm a list of problems and then guide them through a process of choosing one to focus on. If the class generates a list, you can ask them to vote on which is the most important and keep dropping the ones with the least votes. Each student gets one vote on each round of voting.

Then address the problem as follows:

Ask, What's the problem? Give the students a chance to talk about the problem and how it affects them. As students speak about the problem, encourage others in the class to listen with full presence and awareness, give the speaker focused attention, fully take in what she/he is saying, and listen for underlying needs or concerns.

Brainstorm solutions. The guidelines for brainstorming are: Set a time limit of several minutes. Encourage the group to put out lots of ideas. Record them on a chart or the chalkboard. Don't discuss or judge any idea. The ideas don't need to be "realistic"; sometimes even a "crazy" idea has a germ of wisdom that can lead to a creative solution.

Choose one. Discuss the ideas. Talk about the consequences of carrying out various ideas. Which have the best chance of working to solve the problem? Guide the class through a process of choosing one to try.

Do it! The only way we'll know for sure if it's a good idea is to try it. Set a time limit—long enough to give the idea a good trial, short enough to limit the damage if the idea doesn't work.

Evaluate. When the time limit is up, usually in a week or so, meet to see how effective the idea has been in addressing the problem. In some cases, you may need to tinker with the idea to make it fully effective. In other cases, you may decide to go back to the drawing board. If the idea worked, congratulations! Now you can move on to tackle another problem.

When you're done, debrief with the students. How was this process for you? Do you think we came up with a good solution? Would you recommend using the process again?

> **Note to the teacher:**
> If you and the class find the process useful, have class meetings for problem solving on a regular basis or use ABCDE problem solving whenever problems come up. Your students will be applying the 4Rs skills they're learning to solve real life problems.

Balancing

Ask students to stand. Explain that in this activity they are going to find different ways to balance. Have students begin by standing on one leg. Then see what happens when you

- bend the knee of your standing leg
- raise and lower the lifted foot
- raise arms overhead, in front of you, to the side, or one arm to the front and one to the back

Encourage students to pay attention to their breathing as they balance. For some people, focusing their gaze on a fixed point on a wall in front of them or on the floor helps them to balance.

Closing

Lead the class in the following cheer:

> ABCDE you see
> Problem solved by you and me!

Additional Activities

Make time for silence

During this time the lights are off. No writing, drawing, reading, no gadgets. Just sitting. Encourage students to put their hands on their knees. Students can close their eyes if they want. You can tell them that they can let their minds use the silence as they wish. Or you can suggest ways they might use the silence. For example,

- Practice abdominal breathing (introduced in Unit 2)
- Simply pay attention to your breathing
- Pay attention to sounds you hear in your mind, take yourself to a peaceful place
- Recall a time you had fun
- Recall something you like to do

After the time of silence, ask for a couple of volunteers to share where their minds went during the time. Make time for silence every day, preferably at the same time, such as after lunch or recess or the first and last actions of the day.

By giving students the opportunity to experience time for silence on a daily basis, you'll be instilling a habit that will serve them well for the rest of their lives.

Consider having your students keep a 4Rs journal

Writing (drawing for younger students) is an excellent way to reinforce and consolidate learning. A journal enables students to put all of their Book Talk writing in one place. You can also give them a few minutes after each 4Rs lesson to jot down a few thoughts about what they're taking away or how they're planning to use what they've just learned. If a student tries a new skill, s/he might want to write about what happened. Did it bring a positive result? If a student is stuck in a conflict with someone, s/he might want to do some writing to sort it out and imagine some solutions. You can give them standard journals and encourage them to decorate them.

By having students keep journals, you will be introducing them to a habit or practice that can serve them well the rest of their lives.

Class meetings for problem solving

In this kind of class meeting the teacher empowers students, facilitating a process by which students apply the skills they're developing through 4Rs lessons to real-life situations in the classroom and the school. By the time you reach Unit 5, your students should have the foundational skills (managing feelings, listening, assertiveness) to be good problem solvers. Also, Unit 5 introduces the ABCDE problem-solving model, an approach children can easily grasp. A free downloadable copy of Morningside Center's comprehensive guide, *Class Meetings for Problem Solving*, is available by request.

Related Books

Onion John by Joseph Krumgold. In this chapter book, a young boy befriends a homeless eccentric. The townspeople don't want to eject Onion John, but they do think they know what's best for him, and they want to build him a new home.

Paul Revere's Ride by Henry Wadsworth Longfellow, illust. by Ted Rand. A story poem, although the conflict is not solved peacefully.

Pish, Posh, Said Hieronymous Bosch by Nancy Willard, illustrators, Dianne Dillon and Leo Dillon. The famous painter's housekeeper has had it with the mess and weird creatures in the house. However, after she quits, she finds that she misses it all.

While Standing on One Foot by Nina Jaffe and Steve Zeitlin

Unit 5: Problem Solving — Grade 3

Handout 1 • Unit 5

Copyright © 1984 Sarah Pirtle. A Gentle Wind, publishers. Albany, N.Y. BMI.
Used by permission.

A B C D E
Problem Solving Method

Ask, What's the problem?

Brainstorm solutions.

Choose one.

Do it!

Evaluate. After about a week, check in to see how the solution is working.

Blank by design.

3

Unit 6 Theme

Celebrating Diversity & Countering Bullying and Discrimination

Unit 6 Book Selection

ONE by Kathryn Otoshi
KO KIDS BOOKS, BLUE DOT PRESS, 2008

Activities

- Face to Face
- A Time I Felt Different
- Family Banners
- Prejudice and Discrimination
- It's Not Fair!
- Quick thinking
- Dealing with Bullying
- Things Bullies Do
- What We Can Do
- Think Differently
- Reporting vs. Tattling
- Additional Activities

Introduction

We live in a multi-cultural, multi-racial society, but even if we lived in a mono-cultural one, we would discover numerous differences among us.

In this unit, students will look at the ways that everyone is different while at the same time being part of the human community. They will read stories in which characters are targeted for being "different." In some stories, the community realizes after it is too late how it could have been enriched if it had accepted the person. In other stories, characters gain inner strength to stand up to being targeted, while in others the community bands together against those who target the individual. The key point is that we are all different, and that is totally OK. We do not need to feel bad about ourselves because we don't seem to fit a norm. We do not need to make ourselves feel superior by putting someone else down. Our classroom and our larger community are stronger and better because we each bring different strengths to them.

There is no place in our classroom or in society for putting down or mistreating others because they are "different." Research shows that children as young as three and four can see differences and pick up cues about responding from the older people around them. The lessons for pre-K through first grade focus on acknowledging similarities and differences among people and accepting them.

In grades two through five, the lessons continue to emphasize acknowledging and celebrating diversity. In these grades we also address the shadow side of diversity, the ways in which difference is used as an excuse for teasing and bullying. Teasing and bullying exist in classrooms where everyone is the same age and from the same ethnic group. The "differences" can be height, weight, wearing glasses, gender, hair color, having the "wrong" clothes, or social class, to name a few. In multi-ethnic classrooms, aggressors may seize on perceived racial differences.

Whatever reasons aggressors pick for targeting individuals, not one is valid. Our school communities need to be based on respect for all. Bullying has no place in the school. In grades two through five, we define bullying and identify four roles people play in bullying situations:

- Aggressor
- Target
- Bystander
- Ally

As we address bullying in the older grades, teachers need to keep in mind that not all aggression is bullying. A fight between two evenly matched opponents may be against school rules, but it is not bullying. A shouting match between two verbally adept students may be unpleasant and unnecessary, but it is not bullying. **Bullying always involves a real or perceived power imbalance**. The bully does it because he or she can. Bullies don't pick on people who will resist successfully. We define bullying as a repeated pattern of aggression intended to hurt another person, either physically or emotionally. It's not only physical: words do hurt. In addition, with the Internet, bullying can be carried on from a distance and anonymously.

This unit will begin to give students tools to understand and accept difference and to combat bullying. Students in the older grades will learn that in addition to aggressors and targets, there are bystanders and allies. For every bully there are many bystanders. They are literally people who are on the scene, standing by. Every bystander has the potential to become an ally, either by offering support to the target afterward, standing up to the bully, or getting help from a trusted adult. Ultimately, it's the bystanders, not the bullies, who have the power — if they choose to use it.

Studies show that students have very little confidence in adults to help them in such situation, and, unfortunately, they are right. Too many adults either don't see the bullying in front of their eyes or don't understand how devastating bullying is to the target and how harmful it is to the learning environment.

Bullies often defend their actions with such phrases as, "I was just kidding" or "Can't you take a joke?" Of course, there is teasing among friends, but friends stop at or just after they cross the line. Bullies don't. Adults are not always able to distinguish between playful teasing and harmful teasing.

Although the legal ramifications of bullying are not covered in this unit, teachers should be aware that many states have anti-harassment and anti-bullying legislation. When targets or their families have sued, school districts have been held liable for not preventing or stopping bullying that has caused the target to suffer emotional damage, transfer to another school, or commit suicide. In addition, both students and teachers need to know what the discipline code for their school district is. Students may not realize how stiff the penalties can be for bullying.

Unit 6: Diversity — Grade 3

In this unit

	Ideas	Skills
Literacy	<ul><li>Stories have characters</li><li>Characters in a story can stand for a feeling or thought; they are symbols</li><li>Sometimes we can use stories to understand our own lives</li><li>Words and pictures together can tell a story</li><li>Stories usually have conflict in them</li><li>Stories can inspire people to take action to make the world a place where all are treated with respect</li></ul>	<ul><li>Identifying the main idea</li><li>Predicting</li><li>Asking questions</li><li>Expressing ideas clearly</li><li>Providing evidence to back up one's assertions</li><li>Listening</li><li>Seeing connections between a story and one's life</li></ul>
Social and Emotional Learning	<ul><li>All people are similar to other people in some ways and different in other ways</li><li>All people deserve respect</li><li>It is not OK to make fun of or bully people who are different from you</li><li>Bullying is harmful and wrong and has no place in a caring community</li><li>Allies and bystanders can be helpful in supporting the targeted person and in stopping the bullying</li><li>One person can make a difference by inspiring and mobilizing others</li></ul>	<ul><li>Identifying similarities and differences</li><li>Sharing about our families</li><li>Recognizing prejudice and discrimination</li><li>Generating ideas for changing things that are unfair</li><li>Standing up for oneself and others in bullying situations</li></ul>

ONE, by Kathryn Otoshi
KO KIDS BOOKS, BLUE DOT PRESS, 2008.

SUMMARY

Round, amiable Blue was a "quiet color," who liked "looking up at the sky" or "floating on waves," but also enjoyed "splashing in rain puddles." Sometimes he wanted to be sunny like his friend Yellow or bright like his friend Green or regal (read "dignified") like his friend Purple or extroverted like Orange, but "overall, he liked being Blue," The only problem was Red, who flattened Blue's self-image by boasting about how great his own color is ("Red is hot. Blue is not."). At such times, Blue felt like a puddle rather than a bouncy blob. His friends comforted him, but never when the actual attack was happening. They, too, were afraid of Red, who was much bigger. In fact, each time Red said something mean and no one spoke up, Red got "bigger. . .and bigger. . .and bigger" until he grew "so big that everyone was afraid of him."

And now he "picked on all the colors," making everyone feel "a little blue."

Then along came One, a gray meld of colors who had "a different shape with bold strokes and squared corners" (that is, the shape of the number 1 rather than the circularity of the other colors). Despite his differentness, he fit in because he made the other colors laugh. But Red couldn't stand being upstaged. "Stop laughing!" he roared. All the colors stopped, except for One, who said, "No." Red was furious, but since One didn't back down, Red rolled away. One rallied the others, urging them to "stand up and say, No." Yellow agreed, saying "Me Two!" Green agreed, saying "Me Three!" Purple agreed saying, "Me Four!" Orange agreed, saying "Me Five!"

Enraged, Red decided to pick on the color that had always backed down in the past. But watching the other colors, Blue had decided he "wanted to count" too. He defended himself without demeaning Red: "Red can be really Hot. . .but Blue can be super Cool." For the first time, Red became physical and tried to flatten Blue. The others stood up to Red and said, "No!" Red began to feel small and started to roll away. Blue offered a face-saving gambit. "Can Red be hot…AND Blue be cool?" Red stopped, as One called out, "Red can count too." Red became 7, and the group shouted, "Everyone counts!"

"Then Red laughed and joined in the fun."

COMMENT

The author uses bright colors and a simple story line to show how one person can make a difference and inspire others to stand up and be counted against bullies. We can talk about being firm, about respecting others, and about being assertive without demeaning others. We can remember times when we were inspired by one person's actions to make the world better. We can introduce the literary device of similes (But One stood up straight like an arrow and said "No!") and double meanings for words (("Blue . . . .wanted to count") and have fun creating our own.

We can talk about what we have in common and how we are different in interesting ways ("bold strokes and squared corners"). We can introduce the roles in a bullying situation — aggressor, target, bystander, and ally — and discuss the power bystanders can muster if they join together to become allies for the target. We can write our own stories about the power of one joined by others who count.

In an interview on the Web, the author says that she started the book as a way to talk about diversity. As she learned more about bullying, she realized both that it is always important for children to seek adult help and that standing up to a bully doesn't mean bullying the bully. Thus, she changed her original ending, which had Red leaving the group. In addition, she speaks of her own experience as an Asian in a classroom of almost all European heritage students. She remembers another Asian student who did not speak English well and who was bullied. She regrets not having stood up to help that student and wonders whether she could have changed the dynamic in her classroom. We can ask our students to find stories from their own relatives and other adults around them about bullying.

Book Talk

READ ALOUD

Previewing the book

Show the students the cover of the book. What do they see? What feelings or thoughts do they have as they look at the cover? Ask them to notice the colors. Those colors will be important in the story. Show them the back cover. What do they see there? Ask why they think that a book about how we're all different and about bullying would be called *One*. If you think there will be any unfamiliar words or phrases — such as hot-headed, regal, squared, blew a fuse, take a stand, stopped in his tracks — you may want to go over them with the students either before or after reading the story.

Reading and responding to the story

Read the story through once. Ask the students to turn and talk with a partner about anything they'd like to say about the book. What interested them?

Deepening students' understanding of the story

Elicit from the class an account of what happens in the story in their own words. Ask, What is the story mainly about? The story is about appreciating diversity and about bullying, although the word bullying is never used. Some students may see that Red is a bully. If not, you can bring in the concept.

Tape a piece of chart paper to the wall and write the word "bullying" in the middle of it. Ask students to share their free associations with the word "bullying" and chart their responses. Continue for a few minutes while interest remains high. When you have a good number of words that students associate with bullying, draw lines from "bullying" to the words, creating a web. Ask the students if they want to make any comments or observations about the web.

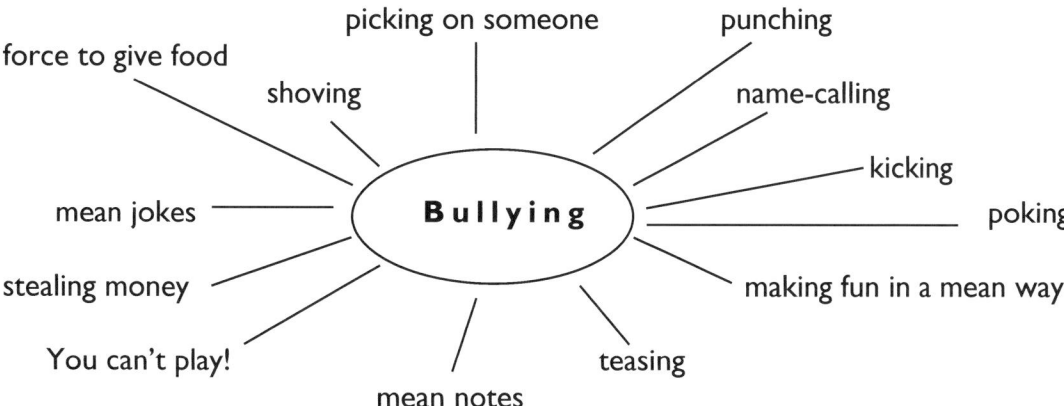

Ask the students, What is bullying? Elicit that bullying is picking on someone again and again (as Red did to Blue), threatening the person, sometimes hurting them or forcing them to do things they don't want to do.

To clarify the definition of bullying in the students' minds, ask them if it's bullying when two friends get into a fight.

Ask questions and elicit examples until students are clear that bullying is a pattern of repeated meanness against a person who is less powerful (often smaller or less popular) than the person doing the bullying.

Connecting the book to students' lives

Ask the students to pair up and share stories of times they have experienced bullying or seen someone being bullied. Tell them not to use names but to describe to their partner what happened. Give them a couple minutes each way to do this. As during other discussions in The 4Rs curriculum that may raise strong emotions, encourage students to take a few abdominal breaths together (see Unit 2, Lesson 3, page 28) before and after each speaker. Deep breathing is a way for students to calm themselves and bring full awareness to their own emotions and those of their partner.

Call on a couple of volunteers to share their stories with the class. Remind them not to use names.

Discussion: As the volunteers tell their stories, ask questions such as the following:
- Did anyone try to help the person being bullied?
- Did anyone try to stop the bully?
- Were any adults aware of what was happening? Did they do something to help?

- How did the person doing the bullying feel? How did the person being bullied feel? How did you feel as someone watching it?

As the teacher, you may want to share a personal experience, perhaps from when you were the students' ages.

Writing: Ask the students to draw a picture based on the experience with bullying that they shared with their partner. They can write a one or two sentence caption for their drawing.

ROLE-PLAY

Divide your class into three or four groups of about seven students each. Provide swatches of colored cloth or pieces of construction paper to represent the characters in *One*. Ask each group to prepare a skit based on the story. Explain that each group will need to decide who will play One and who will play Red and who will play the others. Then they will need to work out their skit. The book is available if they need to check it. You are available to help them as well. Give them 15 or 20 minutes to rehearse their skits before presenting them to the class. After each skit, lead the class in applause.

After each skit, ask the students how they felt playing their parts. After all three skits have been presented, send the talking piece around for students to share their take-aways from the book *One*.

Applied Learning

Lesson 1

Objectives

Students will
- notice similarities and differences between themselves and their classmates;
- become more aware of similarities and differences among people in general
- recall a time when they felt different

Materials

- Agenda on chart paper or the chalkboard

Gathering: Attribute Linking

Students stand in an area of the classroom where they can move around. When you call out a preference or attribute, those who have the preference or attribute in common find each other and stand together.

For example, if you call out, "Favorite season of the year," the students whose favorite season is spring will find each other and stand together, while students who prefer winter, fall, or summer will do the same.

Once the students are standing with others who share the same preference or attribute, you can ask each group to say something about why they're standing there or what it's like to be in that group: Would someone who likes spring give your reasons? How about those who like winter? And so on.

Continue with other attributes or preferences, such as favorite day of the week, favorite month of the year, favorite TV show, favorite sport. An interesting attribute is age order of children in the family (oldest, middle, youngest, only child), When the students are standing with others who have the same age order , you can ask each group, What's it like to be [oldest, youngest, etc.] What do you like about it? What's challenging?

Check agenda

Go over the objectives and the agenda.

Face to Face*

Partners will find out what they have in common and how they are different.

Assign partners and have them stand or sit facing each other. They have three minutes to find out and jot down five ways they differ from their partners and five characteristics they have in common. Encourage them to do this in silence so that they approach the activity with mindful and respectful attention.

Have everyone change partners and repeat the exercise.

With the entire class, list typical similarities and differences on the board.

Discuss: What were some of the differences? Were there similarities that went along with differences (for example, most people have hair, but hair has different colors and textures)? Which differences are most important? Which are least important? Did you notice mostly physical characteristics? What other characteristics could you have noticed? What features are most people born with? Which can they change? How?

* From *Creative Conflict Resolution* by William J. Kreidler. © 1984 by Good Year Books.
Used by permission of Pearson Education, Inc.

A time I felt different

A central message of *One* is that it takes one person to stand up to injustice, but it is more effective if others join in. Blue, for instance, could have stood up for himself, but if others hadn't backed him, he would still have suffered from Red's bullying.

Sometimes we don't stand up for ourselves because we don't want to call attention to the way we are "different." We may not stand up for someone who is different because we are afraid that the bully will pick on us next.

Now have the students work with a partner, and take turns talking about "a time I felt different." You can model this by sharing a time when you felt different, preferably when you were the same age as the students. Encourage partners to take a few deep breaths together before and after speaking. Remind the students that whatever is said in the pairs is confidential. Nothing should be shared unless the person agrees to it.

Give several volunteers a chance to share their experience with the group. After a student describes an experience of feeling different, you might ask if anything happened to change the situation so that the student felt accepted and became part of the group. Did anyone have a positive experience with feeling different?

Evaluation

Ask, What did you learn from today's workshop? What new thoughts or ideas came to you? What did you enjoy about the activities we did today? Give several students a chance to share their thoughts with the group.

Closing

Ask students to turn and talk with a partner about something they are thankful for. This could be someone in their family, a friend, a pet or something they like to do. Ask a couple of volunteers to share what they're thankful for with the group.

Lesson 2

Objectives

Students will
- identify values, activities, and traditions important in their families
- learn about values, activities, and traditions important in their classmates' families

Materials
- Agenda on chart paper or the chalkboard
- Drawing paper for all students
- Markers or crayons for all students

Gathering

Ask students to pair up and share something they like to do with their family. Ask for a couple of volunteers to share with the group.

Check agenda

Go over the objectives and the agenda.

Family Banners

Prepare students for this activity by sharing some information about your family. For example, you might talk about your family when you were growing up or your family now; you might talk about your immediate family and your extended family; you might share something about your cultural background—where your ancestors came from and why they came to this country; and you might talk a bit about some values that were important in your family as you were growing up.

> **Note** that some students may not be living with their birth families and may not have much information about them. They can talk about the family they have now.

Ask for volunteers to share similar information about their families. You might find something to serve as a play microphone and call several students to come up one at a time for a brief interview. Questions might include: Who's in your immediate family? Who is in your extended family? What are some things your family likes to do together? Does your family have special celebrations or traditions? Did you, your parents, your grandparents or your long-ago ancestors come to our country from another country?

After completing several brief interviews with students, pass out drawing paper and markers or crayons. Tell the students you want each of them to make a "family banner" by writing their family name in the center and drawing things or writing words that represent what's important in their family (activities, values, celebrations, traditions, favorite places, etc.). While the students are working, make your own family banner.

On another day, after the students have completed their banners, give students a chance to share their banners with the group and talk a bit about them. To ensure that students pay good attention to each other, you may want to do the sharing of the banners in several sittings.

Evaluation

Have the students work with a partner. Ask, What's one thing you learned from our workshop today? After they've had a chance to talk in pairs, ask for several volunteers to share their thoughts with the group.

Closing

Send high fives around the circle.

Lesson 3

Objectives

Students will
- identify things that are unfair;

Unit 6: Diversity — Grade 3

- define prejudice and discrimination and give examples from their own experience;
- generate ideas for standing up to unfair treatment directed at them or someone else.

Materials

- A brightly colored balloon
- Agenda on chart paper or the chalkboard
- A talking piece
- Chart paper with the definitions of prejudice and discrimination, as follows:
  - Prejudice is a negative attitude or opinion not based on knowledge
  - Discrimination is action (doing something) based on prejudice

Gathering: This is a _____ !

The students pass the balloon around the circle. Upon receiving the balloon, students use their imaginations to think of what it might be (besides a balloon). For example: "This is an idea" "This is the biggest piece of hard candy I've ever seen" "This is a cloud"

Check agenda

Go over the objectives and the agenda.

It's not fair!

Show students the two-page spread depicting Red picking on Blue. ("Red was a hot head. He liked to pick on Blue. 'Red is a great color,' he'd say. 'Red is hot. Blue is not.'")

Is it fair the way Red is picking on Blue?

Ask, What do you see or experience in your life that you find unfair? Send the talking piece around for students to describe things they find unfair.

Prejudice and Discrimination

Explain that today we're going to explore a kind of unfairness called prejudice and discrimination. Ask, what is prejudice? Elicit the students' thinking.

Referring to your chart with the definitions of prejudice and discrimination, explain that sometimes people have negative attitudes toward people different from themselves. Without even knowing the person, they assume they won't like the person. This is called prejudice. Prejudice is a negative attitude or opinion that is not based on knowledge.

You might mention (or read them) the Dr. Seuss book *Green Eggs and Ham*, which your students may be familiar with. The character in that story says again and again that he doesn't like green eggs and ham. Finally, when he tries them, he actually likes them. His original opinion was formed without knowledge. That's an example of prejudice. People can also have prejudice about other people.

In the story, Red is prejudiced against Blue. "Red is hot. Blue is not." Though the book doesn't provide background on the relationship between Red and Blue, it's a fair assumption that Red never took the trouble to get to know Blue. He was prejudiced against Blue from the start.

Ask if the students can think of other examples of prejudice. Have they ever had the experience of having a negative attitude toward somebody at first, but then changing their mind when they got to know the person? Elicit examples from the students. Share an example from your own life if you think it would be helpful.

Again referring to your chart, explain that discrimination is <u>doing</u> something based on prejudice. If you are prejudiced toward somebody — if you have a negative attitude toward them because they are different from you in some way — and you do mean things to them, that's discrimination. That's what happens in the story. Red is prejudiced against Blue and acts on that prejudice, mistreating Blue by putting Blue down and making Blue feel bad. Driven by prejudice against Blue, Red bullies Blue. Red discriminates against Blue.

Ask, What are other examples of discrimination — of someone doing mean things to another person because they are different in some way? Elicit examples from several volunteers. Encourage the students to think of examples from their own lives.

Are prejudice and discrimination fair? What effect do they have on people? When things happen that are unfair, either to us or to someone else, what should we try to do?

Quick Thinking: Standing up against things that are unfair

In "Quick Thinking," you will describe a situation to the class; and then students, working in pairs, have a minute or two to come up with an idea for addressing it. When the time is up, the pairs share their idea with the group. The aim is to generate lots of ideas and get people thinking, not necessarily to come with one "best" approach.

Ask students to pair up. Remind them that in the story, One came into a situation that was unfair. How was it unfair? Call on a couple of volunteers to share their thoughts. What did One do? Elicit that he stood up straight like arrow and said "No!"

Explain that in this "Quick Thinking" exercise, they're going to work with their partners to think of ideas for standing up, as One did, when they see something unfair.

Below are examples of the kinds of situations you might present to the students for "quick thinking." Choose or invent other situations that you think will be relevant to your students <u>but are not currently being experienced by anyone in your class.</u> See note below!

- A group of boys is playing basketball. A girl asks to play and is told, "No! Girls aren't any good at basketball! Go play jump rope with the other girls."
- A boy is a talented performer and is taking ballet lessons. Some boys are teasing him and calling him a sissy.

- A new girl in the school doesn't speak English very well. (She has recently come from another country.) Kids are making fun of her, mimicking her way of speaking, laughing, and saying "You talk funny. Go back where you came from"

> **Note**: Avoid choosing situations that will put one of your students in a painful spot. The aims of the activity are 1) to show students that discrimination is wrong, and 2) to make the point that when we see things that are unfair, we need to do what we can to stop the mistreatment. Don't use the activity to address a particular situation that's happening in your classroom. To address a particular situation, confer with your school's guidance counselor and address it privately with those involved.

After students have talked in pairs for one to two minutes about one of the situations, call on several pairs of students to share their thinking. Use the play microphone to interview the students. Ask, What kind of prejudice is at work in this situation? What are your thoughts for stopping this mistreatment based on prejudice?

After students of each pair have shared their ideas, open up the discussion for comments and feedback from the class.

If time allows, repeat with other situations.

Evaluation

Can you see yourself standing up against something unfair, perhaps using some of the ideas we came up with in "Quick Thinking"? Why? Why not? Send the talking piece around for students to share their thoughts.

Closing

End with a round of applause

Lesson 4

Objectives

Students will
- see a skit in which two boys talk about being bullied
- share their ideas about how to stop the bullying

Materials

- Copies of the handout, "Bullying Script," for two students who will play the characters
- Chart paper or white board and markers
- The agenda on chart paper or the white board
- A talking piece

Grade 3 — One

> **Note**: Before the workshop begins, choose two students to play the characters in the skit.

Gathering: Deep Breathing

Turn off the lights and enjoy a few minutes of silence with your students. Begin by leading them in several cycles of deep breathing, as introduced in Unit 2. Then introduce three minutes of silence by asking them, as they sit silently, to listen carefully to everything they hear.

When the time is up, call on several students to share what they heard.

Check agenda

Go over the objectives and the agenda

Dealing with bullying

Remind the students that after hearing the story *One*, they discussed bullying and defined it as picking on someone over and over, trying to hurt them or force them to do things they don't want to do.

Explain that two students are now going to act out a situation involving bullying. After the skit, the class will share ideas about how to deal with the situation.

Introduce the skit by explaining that two third graders are talking in a corner of the school playground about a fifth-grader who has been mistreating them.

> **Note**: Make sure that the names you choose for the characters in the skit are not the names of students in your class.

Student A: I hate _____ [name]

Student B: Yeah. He's really mean.

Student A: I just had to give him my candy. He said he'd beat me up after school if I didn't.

Student B: I know. Yesterday he told me he'd get me on the way home if I didn't give him my cookies from lunch. He thinks he's big and bad because he's in fifth grade.

Student A: Yeah. And I don't like the way he bosses us around. Remember last week when we were in line for the drinking fountain and he cut right in front of us and pushed us out of the way?

Unit 6: Diversity   Grade 3

Freeze the action at this point. Ask, What's going on here? Have any of you ever experienced a situation like this or seen it happening to someone else? Call on a couple of students to share their experiences.

Now ask, What should the boys do? Ask students to pair up and share their thoughts with a partner. After students have a couple of minutes to talk in pairs, ask each pair to share their ideas with the group. Chart their responses.

Evaluation

What do you think of the ideas the class came up with? Could you see using any of them to deal with a real-life bully? Why? Why not? You might ask for a show of hands for each idea to see which one(s) the students favor.

Closing

Send the talking piece around for students to share one thing they're looking forward to.

Lesson 5

Objectives

Students will
- identify the forms bullying can take
- think of ways to help when they become aware that someone is being bullied
- discuss the difference between reporting and snitching (tattling)

Materials Needed
- A talking piece
- Today's agenda posted on chart paper or the white board
- Chart paper with the heading, "Things Bullies Do"
- Chart paper with the heading, "What We Can Do"
- Two signs, one labeled "Strongly Agree" and the other, "Strongly Disagree," for the Think Differently activity

Gathering

Send the talking piece around for students to tell a brief story about a time they helped someone. Model the activity by telling about time you helped someone.

Check agenda

Go over the objectives and the agenda.

Things bullies do

Red was acting like a bully when he picked on Blue and the other colors again and again. How did he pick on Blue and the others? What exactly did he do? Elicit that Red gave Blue put-downs. Red said things that made Blue feel bad. Red also bossed Blue and the other colors around. For example, Red told them stop laughing—and they did.

Call students' attention to the chart with the heading, "Things Bullies Do." Chart the two bullying behaviors discussed so far: "Putting people down" and "Bossing people around."

Ask, What are other things do bullies do? If students need prompting, remind them of the skit in the previous lesson and add "Forcing people to give money" to the list.

Elicit other things for the list, including "Teasing" "Excluding people" "Threatening" "Hitting" "Pushing." Remind students that hitting and pushing and teasing are not always bullying. It's only bullying if it's aimed at one person and repeated again and again.

After completing the list, review the items with the students and ask if anyone has anything they want to say about the chart. Call on a couple of students to share their thoughts.

What we can do

When we see someone being bullied, we have a choice. We can join the bully. We can say to ourselves, "It's none of my business," and do nothing. Or we can try to help.

Ask, What do you think would be "The 4Rs choice"? What choice would One want us to make?

Assuming we choose to try to help, what can we do? Ask, What did One do? Elicit that One told Red "No!" So that's one thing we can do. We can tell the bully to stop. Record that on the chart labeled "Things We Can Do."

Ask the students pair up and share with their partners other ideas of things we can do.

Give the students a couple of minutes to talk in pairs. Then call on each pair to share their ideas. Then add their ideas to the list of 'Things We Can Do."

The list might include the following:

- Walk up to the bully and say "No! Stop! What you're doing is wrong!"
- Get some friends together and ask the bully to stop
- Make friends with the person who is being bullied
- Tell a teacher
- Tell a parent
- Tell the guidance counselor

Think Differently

Using the ideas on the list of "Things We Can Do," engage students in the Think Differently activity, introduced in Unit 1. One side of the room is Strongly Agree and the opposite end is Strongly Disagree. Turn each item on the list into a statement, as follows: "The best thing to do when we see someone being bullied is _____." Students go to the appropriate place in the room depending on whether they strongly agree, strongly disagree, or are somewhere in the middle.

When students have chosen where to stand, ask those in each location to explain their thinking. Encourage lively discussion. The aim is not to arrive at the "right" choice but to explore the pros and cons of each choice. There is no right or wrong answer as each situation is different.

Reporting vs. Tattling

Point out that some students have suggested that the best way to help in a bullying a situation is to tell an adult. Ask, Is that *tattling* on someone? Call on several students to share their thoughts. Engage the class in discussion about this crucial issue.

In summary: Help the students understand the difference between tattling on someone and reporting a situation in which is someone is getting hurt. Tattling is telling on someone with the intention of getting them in trouble and winning points with an adult. Reporting a bullying situation is about stopping harmful abuse of another person.

Tell the students that bullying has no place in our classroom community and you want to know if anything like that is going on. As an adult it's your responsibility to ensure that the classroom is a safe place for everybody, and you need their help: If they see something, they should say something.

Evaluation

Ask, Is it easy or hard to stand up for someone being targeted for bullying? Why? Do you think it took courage for One to stand up to Red? Why? Why not?

Ask students to pair up and share their thoughts with a partner. After the pair-share, call on a couple of students to share their thoughts with the class.

Closing: Balancing

Repeat the "Balancing" activity from Unit 5, Lesson 3, in which students have to keep their balance while standing on one foot. But this time have students find a partner and create a balanced position involving both people, each standing on one foot. Partners may support and steady each other by holding hands, leaning against each other's shoulders, balancing back to back, touching knees, etc.

Ask for a few volunteers to demonstrate their balanced position. Discuss: What is the connection between this activity and helping someone who is being bullied?

End with a round of applause to celebrate people who help others.

Additional Activities

Make time for silence

During this time the lights are off. No writing, drawing, reading, no gadgets. Just sitting. Encourage students to put their hands on their knees. Students can close their eyes if they want. You can tell them that they can let their minds use the silence as they wish. Or you can suggest ways they might use the silence. For example,

- Practice abdominal breathing (introduced in Unit 2)
- Simply pay attention to your breathing
- Pay attention to sounds you hear in your mind, take yourself to a peaceful place
- Recall a time you had fun
- Recall something you like to do

After the time of silence, ask for a couple of volunteers to share where their minds went during the time. Make time for silence every day, preferably at the same time, such as after lunch or recess or the first and last actions of the day.

By giving students the opportunity to experience time for silence on a daily basis, you'll be instilling a habit that will serve them well for the rest of their lives.

Consider having your students keep a 4Rs journal

Writing (drawing for younger students) is an excellent way to reinforce and consolidate learning. A journal enables students to put all of their Book Talk writing in one place. You can also give them a few minutes after each 4Rs lesson to jot down a few thoughts about what they're taking away or how they're planning to use what they've just learned. If a student tries a new skill, s/he might want to write about what happened. Did it bring a positive result? If a student is stuck in a conflict with someone, s/he might want to do some writing to sort it out and imagine some solutions. You can give them standard journals and encourage them to decorate them.

By having students keep journals, you will be introducing them to a habit or practice that can serve them well the rest of their lives.

Class meetings for problem solving

In this kind of class meeting the teacher empowers students, facilitating a process by which students apply the skills they're developing through 4Rs lessons to real-life situations in the classroom and the school. By the time you reach Unit 5, your students should have the foundational skills (managing feelings, listening, assertiveness) to be good problem solvers. Also, Unit 5 introduces the ABCDE problem-solving model, an approach children can easily grasp. A free downloadable copy of Morningside Center's comprehensive guide, *Class Meetings for Problem Solving*, is available by request.

Related Books

Abuela's Weave by Omas S. Castaneda

Amazing Grace by Mary Hoffman, illustrated by Caroline Binch

Blubber by Judy Blume

Charlotte's Web by E. B. White

The Emperor's New Clothes by Hans Christian Andersen

The First Woman Doctor by Rachel Baker

My Name Is Maria Isabel by Alma Flor Ada

Open Minds to Equality: A Sourcebook of Learning Activities to Affirm Diversity and Promote Equity, 3rd edition, by Nancy Schniedewind and Ellen Davidson.

The Sneetches by Dr. Seuss

Handout • Unit 6

Script for Bullying Skit

Two third graders are talking in a corner of the school playground about a fifth-grader who has been mistreating them.

Student A: I hate _____!

Student B: Yeah, he's really mean.

Student A: I just had to give him my candy. He said he'd beat me up after school if I didn't.

Student B: I know. Yesterday he told me he'd get me on the way home if I didn't give him my cookies from lunch. He thinks he's big and bad because he's in fifth grade.

Student A: Yeah, and I don't like the way he bosses us around. Remember last week when we were in line for the drinking fountain and he cut right in front of us and pushed us out of the way?

Blank by design.

3

Unit 7 Theme

Making a Difference

Unit 7 Book Selection

Baseball Saved Us by Ken Mochizuki
Lee & Low Books, 1993

Activities

- Reflecting on our year with The 4Rs
- A gift I can give the world [make a pledge]
- Completing our pledges
- Presenting our pledges and getting support from the group
- Additional Activities

Introduction

In this unit we will look at stories of individuals who, working with others, acted courageously to make the world a better place. Across the grades some of the characters are fictional and some are real people. What they have in common is the understanding that we are linked together in our struggles for peace, freedom, and justice.

In each story at each grade level there is an individual who channels his or her fear and anger at injustice to constructive action. That action makes a difference in the lives of others.

The stories of these outstanding individuals are inspiring, but we do not have to be heroes to make a difference. Whenever we help a neighbor, intervene to keep a quarrel from escalating, refuse to rise to the bait of anger, teach someone something useful, give a heartfelt compliment, we are building community and making a difference. Each act may seem isolated, but each builds on others to empower us to act courageously and create peaceful, just communities.

Since this is the last unit of the curriculum, students will reflect on their year with The 4Rs: the stories they've heard, the games they've played, the skills they've learned. The 4Rs teaches leadership skills that will help them make a contribution to the communities they become part of — from the classroom to the world.

In this unit students will also reflect on times they have made a difference for others and identify the strengths they have that enabled them to do so. They will think of something concrete they can do in the here and now to make the world a better place and make a pledge to do it. As they share their pledges with the class, their classmates will let them know that they have the support of their 4Rs friends behind them.

In this unit

	Ideas	Skills
Literacy	• Words and pictures can tell a story • Stories can show us ways to act in our own lives • Stories have characters • Sometimes characters change in the course of a story • Some stories can teach us about important events that have happened in the past	• Summarizing the action • Identifying the main idea • Providing evidence to back up one's assertions • Identifying the personal qualities of characters in a story • Making connections between stories and our lives
Social and Emotional Learning	• We can work together to make the world safer and fairer • Everyone can do something to make a difference • It takes a hopeful attitude and good ideas to make a difference in the world	• Reflecting on past experience and drawing conclusions • Identifying our strengths • Generating ideas • Planning a course of action to make a difference • Making a pledge

Baseball Saved Us, by Ken Mochizuki.
Illustrated by Dom Lee. Lee and Low Books Inc., 1993.

SUMMARY

"One day, my dad looked out at the endless desert and decided then and there to build a baseball field." With that spare sentence the young narrator plunks us into the middle of a story about Japanese Americans interned in a desert camp for the duration of World War II. We learn that the boy's family is in a camp "in the middle of nowhere. . . behind a barbed-wire fence" where soldiers "with guns made sure we stayed there." The boy asks again why they are there. " 'Because,'" his father answers, " 'America is at war with Japan, and the government thinks that Japanese Americans can't be trusted. But it's wrong that we're in here. We're Americans too!' "

The boy thinks back to his life before the Camp. He played baseball then, but not well, and because he was shorter and smaller than the other kids in his school he was "always the last to be picked." Then, after the Japanese attack on Pearl Harbor, "it got even worse." Kids called him names and "nobody talked to me, even though I didn't do anything bad." One day, his parents pick him up from school and tell him that they have to move out of their home fast. They take very little with them and board a bus to a "place where we had to live in horse stalls" before coming to the Camp. Now they are in the desert, sweltering by day, freezing by night, living in barracks with no privacy, using communal latrines, eating with everyone else. His older brother, Teddy, now eats with his own friends. No one is sleeping well because of the noise and discomfort.

"Back home," the boy comments, "the older people were always busy working." But now there was nothing to do. When the boy's father asks Teddy to get him a cup of water, his son snaps, " 'Get it yourself.' " The older men are shocked, and one yells at him for showing such disrespect. Teddy "kicked the crate he was sitting on and walked away." The boy "had never heard Teddy talk to Dad that way before."

That was the straw that pushed the father to create the baseball field. Soon, everyone was helping, including people (presumably of non-Japanese ancestry) from back home who sent supplies. The community pulls together, finding wood for bleachers in a place that has no wood; flooding the earth with water from irrigation ditches to pack down the dirt in the field, sewing uniforms from mattress ticking. Throughout the process, the guard in the tower watches, as he does every day, and the boy comes to think of him as someone who not only guards him like an animal but probably "thought I was no good" as a player. However, the boy admits that playing became easier because most of the kids "were the same size as me." Soon, "there were baseball games all the time." Presumably, these were still male activities, but women were undoubtedly supportive. Grown-ups and kids played. Slowly, the boy's game improves.

Now it's the last game of the season. The other team is winning, three to two at the bottom of the ninth. One of the boy's teammates is on second and there are two outs. He comes up to bat. Part of the crowd cheers him, the other part screams, 'Strike out!'" The boy looks up and sees the guard in the tower. The man is leaning on the rail, "with the blinding sun glinting off his sunglasses. He was always watching, always staring. It suddenly made me mad. "

The boy focuses his energy and his anger. "I was gonna hit the ball past the guardhouse even if it killed me." He makes a home run, sending his team to victory. "I looked up at the tower and the man, with a grin on his face, gave me the thumbs-up sign." But the story doesn't end here.

The war is over and the boy returns home. Most of his friends from Camp didn't go back. "Nobody talked to us on the street, and nobody talked to me at school, either . . . .I had to eat lunch by myself." However, baseball season arrives, and "I was the smallest guy again, but playing baseball in Camp had made me a lot better." The other guys have more respect for him, and when they call him "Shorty" they smile. He is beginning to feel like part of the group. Then he goes to the first game of the season and realizes that no one on his or the other team or in the crowd looks like him. He hears people yelling " 'Jap.' " "I hadn't heard that word since before I went to Camp – it meant they hated me." With people yelling hateful words at him, he loses his confidence and misses the ball twice. But his teammates encourage him: " 'C'mon Shorty, you can do it!' " He starts to focus. Then, when he looks at the pitcher, he sees that the "sun glinted off his glasses...like the guard in the tower." He connects with the ball and it looks "like it was going over the fence." The last frame of the book, also the most colorful picture, shows him being congratulated by his teammates.

COMMENT

What could be more American than a baseball story about an ostracized group that seizes the national pastime to instill the discipline and sense of community that it must have to survive the debilitating and demoralizing experience of the internment camps? We might protest that the ending is too easy, that the problems of racism are not so easily overcome. And that's true. But it is also true that the sports metaphor is an important one and useful as we explore the ways in which a group can sustain itself in the face of adversity. The author, speaking from the perspective of a small boy, does not explore the gender issues here, except to mention that the adults no longer had work to do. Are these adults mainly men? We might imagine that in the early 1940s, the women may not have worked much outside the home and are therefore still engaged in the work they always did, only now under much harsher circumstances. The men's roles have been taken away from them as well as their ability to protect and provide for their families. As the social fabric wears thin, with families crowded into each other's lives, the system of respect begins to break down. When an older son defies his father, it is time for action. Instead of a futile effort to insist on respect, the father sees the need for the community to come together around a common goal. For the purposes of this story, and in fact, in many situations, a sport serves as the glue to keep the group together and as a metaphor for group solidarity, channeling of anger into constructive force, and bringing people together. Baseball is a uniquely American metaphor for diversity, being a team sport that does not necessarily require bulk or height.

As we read the story, we can learn about the backdrop of the war. We can learn the history of the Japanese in America, most of whom had been in their homes for several generations. This may be the first time that many students learn that the United States had camps that, although not death camps as in Germany or prisoner of war camps as in Japan, were certainly prison camps for noncombatants in clear violation of all accepted practices of "civilized" warfare. We might note that Americans of German or Italian heritage, although discriminated against, were rarely subjected to the treatment given Japanese Americans.

Unit 7: Making a difference   Grade 3

We need to find out about the Americans who protested this treatment. There weren't many, but there were some. We need to explore the actions of the people who pressed for an apology from the U.S. government, one that finally came in 1988.

We can discuss prejudice and its complexity. The story tells us that friends from outside sent supplies. Still, these friends didn't support the boy when he returned home. Were they afraid of what other people of European heritage would think of them? We can talk about the anti-Japanese propaganda campaigns and the very real fact that many families probably lost relatives in the war. There was anger at the Japanese that built on already existing prejudice. We can look at images of Asians and Japanese in particular in the media and in literature.

What kind of courage would it have taken for non-Japanese heritage people to reach out to the Japanese Americans? What kind of courage did it take for the Japanese Americans to return to their homes and face people who profited from their land and material goods and to rebuild their lives? Do we have the courage to stand up for ourselves and for others?

We can ask what other ways the community could have held itself together in the camps (religion, ritual, self-government) and find out what people in fact did. We can invite Japanese Americans to talk to the class.

Book Talk

READ ALOUD

Previewing the book

Show the cover of the book and the title page. What do people think the book will be about? What do they notice about the picture? What is different from a normal baseball field? Note that the book is about Japanese Americans almost sixty years ago. Elicit information from the class about what they know about Japanese Americans and about Japan. If there are students of Asian heritage in the class, it could be hurtful to them to have to listen to the misinformation other students may have about them (for instance, many non-Asians categorize people from Japan, China, or Korea as all being the same). The teacher should just give a few facts, showing Japan on the map, noting that there have been Japanese in America for more than 150 years. If there are students of Japanese heritage, would an adult from their families be willing to share information with the class? Read the author's note. Point out the areas mentioned in the note and in the book: Japan, Pearl Harbor, the West Coast, and the deserts.

Reading and responding to the book

Read the book through, pausing only perhaps to explain the attack on Pearl Harbor or something about baseball if there are children who are not familiar with the game. Afterward, ask students to pair up and talk with each other about the story. What struck them about the book? What questions do they have? What do they want to know more about? What do they notice about the pictures (moving from drabness of Camp life to full color in the last frame)? Do the pictures make them think of something that happened in the past?

Deepening students' understanding of the book

Ask the students what they think the themes of the book are? What are some of the things this book is about? Get as many ideas as possible. We are looking in particular at how one person, working with a community, can bring about change. In this case, the father had an idea, enlisted help, and kept the community from disintegrating. In addition, being on the team gave the boy a way to focus his anger and to change his life. He got to be a better player and was able to stand up against prejudice.

Tell the student that there's an important turning point in the story when someone makes a decision that changes things for the better. Who is that someone takes leadership to turn things around? Elicit from the students that it's the father of the boy telling the story. Ask what triggers his decision to get the people in the camp involved in building a baseball field and playing baseball and organizing a tournament? How does doing all this affect the people in the camp?

Elicit students' ideas, then read the story again pausing to encourage student reflection on the father's motivation and the impact of his leadership. Ask the students to identify the qualities the boy's father had that enabled him to make a difference. Elicit that he

- wasn't satisfied with things as they were and wasn't willing to settle for them
- thought of good idea — one that was doable and people in the camp would like
- was able to get people to work together to carry out the idea.

Ask the students to recall the variety of ways people in the camp contribute to carrying out the father's idea. Record students' ideas on chart paper or the white board.

Ask, How does the boy change in the course of the story? Elicit that he becomes a better baseball player and a more confident person. Ask, What helps him hit the home run in the ninth inning of the tournament? Elicit that he channels his anger into increased focus and effort.

Have the students read other books where sports helped a character understand him or herself better or helped change someone's life.

Connecting the book to students' lives

Discussion:
- Ask the students to pair up and talk with a partner about a time when they were part of a team or a group of people who worked together to accomplish something. This could be a sports team as in the story or your family or a club in your afterschool program. What was it like to be on the team? How did the other people treat you? How did you feel about working with the team? What did you like? What didn't you like? Model the activity by telling a story from your own life. After the students have talked in pairs for

a couple of minutes, call on several volunteers to share their stories with the group. Then discuss: What's fun about working with a group? What can be challenging?

and/or

- Send the talking piece around for students to recall a time when they saw something unfair or wrong and decided to take action to change it, as the boy's father did in the story. What was the situation you didn't like? What did you decide to do? What happened? How did it turn out? If some students can't recall a time, they can think of something they find unfair and imagine what they would like to do. Model the activity by telling a story from your own life.

and/or

- When the boy was up at the plate batting, he saw the sun glinting off the sunglasses of the soldier who was always watching, always staring at the people in the camp, and it made him mad. But spurred by the anger he gripped the bat harder and took a couple of practice swings and decided he was going to hit the ball past the guard house—and he did! Ask the students to raise their hands if any of them have ever gotten mad about something and channeled the anger to accomplish something important. Model the activity by telling a story from your own life.

Writing: Ask students to write about a topic they discussed above.

ROLE-PLAY

Divide the class into small groups. In each group the students act out the scene where Teddy talks back to his father. Then they do a second scene in which the father and mother talk to each other about what to do. Discuss: How was it to act out these scenes? Have you ever felt like Teddy? Would most parents have punished Teddy? Why? Why not?

Applied Learning

Lesson 1

Objectives

Students will
- recall the books they've read, the games they've played, and they skills they've practiced in The 4Rs
- identify their favorite and most memorable experiences with the 4rs
- identify important things they have learned from The 4Rs

Grade 3   Baseball Saved Us

Materials Needed
- agenda on chart paper or the chalkboard
- chart paper, masking tape, markers
- copy of the handout "Overview of The 4Rs" (attached)

Gathering: Birthday Line Up

In this cooperative exercise, the students line up in order of their birthdays (January 1 through December 31) by communicating with each other non-verbally. They cannot speak to each other.

Discuss: How did this go? How did you communicate? Did you run into any problems? How did you solve them? What was necessary in order to line up? Are these things necessary for any cooperative venture? What connections do you see between this activity and *Baseball Saved Us*.

Check agenda

Tell the students that in this lesson they're going to take some time to think about their work this year with The 4Rs. They'll recall The 4Rs stories, the games, and the skills.

Our Year with The 4Rs

The father in *Baseball Saved Us* led the way in helping people at the camp come together as a community for the common purpose of playing baseball. Remind the students that at the beginning of the school year we set the goal of creating a supportive classroom community and shared our ideas for doing that. We read the book, *Stone Soup*, in which soup (instead of baseball) provided the impetus for people to come together. To accomplish the father's vision of organizing a baseball tournament in the camp, the people in the camp needed to build a baseball field. Remind the students that to accomplish our vision of a caring classroom community, we agreed to try hard to use put-ups and never put each other down. That was as essential for us to accomplish our vision as building a baseball field was for people in the camp. Ask the students, Have we done that? Thumbs up if you think we've done a pretty good job of putting each other up and eliminating put-downs from our community. Call on a couple of students to share their thoughts.

After we created a vision of how we wanted our classroom to be, we read stories and learned skills to help us make our vision real in the classroom. What are some of the stories we read in The 4Rs? Call on several volunteers to say book titles and characters they remember.

What are some of the skills we practiced? Call on several volunteers to name some of the skills and recall some of the activities we used to practice them.

Distribute copies of the handout "Overview of The 4Rs." Referring to the handout, briefly remind the students of the themes of the seven 4Rs units and the primary skill introduced and practiced in each unit.

Ask students to pair up and share with their partner their favorite 4Rs story. What did they like about it?

With the students now back in a circle, send the talking piece around for students to share their favorite story and why they liked it.

Now ask students to pair up again and share a skill they practiced in The 4Rs that they have found useful. How has it been useful? Have they used it outside of school? How?

Send the talking piece around for students to name 4Rs skills that have made a difference for them. Have they used any of the skills outside of the classroom? If so, ask that they tell the story of their doing that.

Evaluation

What's one thing you learned from The 4Rs that you most want to remember if you forget everything else? Depending on how much time is left, pass the talking piece around, inviting everyone to speak, or have students share with partner, then ask a couple of volunteers to share with the group.

Closing: Rhythm

Students close their eyes and begin to clap in whatever way they want. Have them continue until you call time. In most cases, the cacophony gradually evolves into a discernable rhythm, which demonstrates a natural human tendency toward order and cooperation.

Lesson 2

Objectives

Students will
- recall the gifts the father in *Baseball Saved Us* gave to his community
- identify a gift they can give to the world
- make a pledge to give the gift

Materials Needed

- Hugg-A-Planet
- agenda on chart paper or the chalkboard
- chart paper for recording students' ideas
- copies of the handout "My Gift for the World" for all students

Gathering: Rainstorm *

In this nonverbal activity the students simulate the gradual building and subsiding of a rainstorm. The class needs to be in a circle. Explain that you're going to make a sound with your hands. When you make eye contact with a student, that student should begin imitating your action. Begin by walking over to one of the students, making eye contact, and rubbing your hands together. Move around the circle, continuing to rub your hands together and making eye contact with each student in turn, until all the students are rubbing their hands together. (That's the wind rustling the leaves.) When you come around to the first student, change to snapping your fingers. As you move around the circle, snapping your fingers and making eye contact, each student changes from rubbing hands to snapping fingers. (That's the light pattering of the rain.) Move around the circle for a third time slapping your thighs. (That's the heavy pattering of the rain.) Now repeat the steps in reverse to simulate the subsiding of the storm.

* From *The Friendly Classroom for a Small Planet* by Priscilla Prutzman, et al. New Society Publishers, Gabriola Island, BC, Canada. Copyright © 1988 Children's Creative Response to Conflict, PO Box 271, Nyack, NY 10960. T: (845) 353-1796 / F: (845) 358-4924. Used by permission.

Check agenda

Go over the objectives and the agenda.

A Gift I Can Give to the World

The father in *Baseball Saved Us* came up with a great idea for getting people working together and feeling better. That was his gift to his community.

Explain that you're going to give students the opportunity to think of gifts they'd like to give to the communities they're part of. It could have to do with taking some action, however small, to change something that's unfair in the world. Or they might think about their families, their friends, people they know, people they've read about. How can students contribute to the happiness of these people? How can students make a difference in their lives? The gift should be something concrete—something a student could actually do. To help the students understand, give an example from your own life.

Ask students to pair up and share with their partners some ideas for ways they might make a positive difference for others--gifts they can give to the world. Emphasize once again that they think of concrete things—things they could actually do here and now. Suggest that students do five deep abdominal breaths before talking about their ideas, as a way to help them focus and come up with thoughtful possibilities.

Using the Hugg-A-Planet as a talking piece, invite the students to share their ideas of gifts they might give to the world.

When the students have finished sharing their ideas, say that they are going forth with a year of 4Rs work under their belts. They have many skills and gifts they can give to others. They have thought of some ideas. Now you'd like them to choose one that they'll actually promise to do. You're going to ask them to make a *pledge*.

Ask if they know what a pledge is. Remind them that every morning in most public schools, children recite The Pledge of Allegiance. Have the students stand and recite the Pledge together, even if they've recited it earlier in the day. Ask them if they understand what they're doing when they recite that pledge. What's the meaning of it? Elicit that in reciting the Pledge people are making a promise. That's what a pledge is—it's a promise. In reciting the pledge people are promising to be loyal to our country, the United States, and to its values of liberty and justice.

> **Note to the teacher**: The Pledge of Allegiance was written by a Baptist minister named Francis Bellamy, and first published in 1892 in a popular children's magazine, "The Youth's Companion." It was adopted by Congress as the official national pledge in 1942. The words, "under God," were added in 1954.

Explain that today you want the students to begin work on personal pledges to contribute to the lives of others. They'll be choosing one of the ideas they came up with and promising to do it.

Pass out copies of the handout "My Gift for the World" for students to begin drafting their pledges. Explain that first they'll do a draft. Then they'll revise it, making sure it says clearly what they plan to do and uses correct spelling, etc. When they have completed a good draft, they can copy the pledge on a fresh copy of the handout, and illustrate their pledge.

Model this activity by writing your own pledge before circulating in the classroom to help students decide on a specific thing they will do and to help them with writing and revising.

Once they're happy with their revised draft, give them a fresh pledge sheet and colored markers, pencils, or crayons so that they can begin creating the final version. It's unlikely that they'll finish their pledges in this lesson. They'll have time in the next lesson to finish up.

Evaluation

Pass the Hugg-A-Planet around for students to share one word that names how they're feeling about pledging (promising) to give a gift to the world.

Closing: Tree in a Storm

Ask students if they have ever seen a tree standing in a storm or a strong wind. What parts of the tree moves in a storm? (Branches, leaves) What parts of the tree don't move? (Trunk, roots)

Have students stand in a position with their feet firmly planted on the floor, like the roots of a tree. Have them notice the space around them and where others are standing. Ask them to imagine that they are a tree in an approaching storm. They should move their bodies like a tree as the wind gets stronger (some students may want to close their eyes to imagine this). Say: "At first there is just a gentle breeze blowing the leaves and small branches….Now the wind is getting stronger, and some of the larger branches are moving as well….Now the storm is here – there is rain and strong winds moving the whole upper part of the tree, but the roots are holding firm....The storm is starting to pass, and the wind is slowing down....And now the storm has passed and the wind is blowing softly until....it is still."

Ask for a few volunteers to describe what this was like. Referring back to the book, ask, How were the narrator, his father, and the others in the camp like trees in a storm? How can making a pledge help you to stand firmly, like a tree in a storm, when you try to make change happen in your life?

Lesson 3

Objectives

Students will
- complete their pledges
- identify a quality they'll need in order to carry it out
- receive a symbolic gesture of support from the group

Materials Needed

- Copies of the handout, "My Gift for the World"
- Markers for writing and drawing
- Hugg-A-Planet as a talking piece

Gathering:

Pass the talking piece around for students to appreciate someone in the class or in their life beyond the classroom who has helped them—someone they're grateful for.

Check agenda

Go over the objectives and the agenda.

Completing our pledges

Hand out the drafts of pledges that the students worked on during the last session. Say that during this session they will complete the pledges and share them with the group. If some students have pledges too private to share, they can talk about what it was like for them to create this pledge. Ask whether anyone has questions.

Hand out the drafts and fresh copies of the handout "My Gift for the World" as needed, and give students time to complete a good copy of the pledge they are making.

Ask students to share their pledges in pairs. In addition to describing their pledge to their partner, ask them to think of a personal quality or resource they might need to carry out their pledge. Give them some examples. If they are pledging to help a younger sibling learn to ride a bike, they might need *patience*. If they're going to help a parent with a project around the house, they might need *time*. If they're going to ask grocery store owners to contribute food for a food pantry, they might need *courage*.

Presenting our pledges and getting support from the group

Bring students back in a circle to hold up their pledges and describe the gift they're planning to give to the world. When each student is done, s/he names a personal quality or resource s/he will need to carry out the pledge.

After the student names the quality or resource, lead the students in making a symbolic gesture of support as follows: You and the students stand and direct your attention to the student who has just named the quality or resource s/he will need. Lead the students in raising their arms high up over their heads. Together you and the students bring your arms down pointing toward the student and saying in unison, "We give you _____!" (Name whatever quality or resource the student says s/he will need. Following the examples above, the group might say "We give you patience!" or "We give you time!" or "We give you courage!"

Lead the students in a round of applause to celebrate their commitments to make a difference.

Closing: Group Hug

You and the students stand in a circle. Ask them to hold hands, but not in the usual way. They should hold hands with the next person over on either side, not with the person right next to them. Model this by doing it yourself. Make sure that no person has her or his own arms crossed. With everyone holding hands in this way, lead the students in raising their hands up over their heads and down around their backs. The result is a tight group hug. End with applause for a great year with The 4Rs!

Additional Activities

Make time for silence

During this time the lights are off. No writing, drawing, reading, no gadgets. Just sitting. Encourage students to put their hands on their knees. Students can close their eyes if they want. You can tell them that they can let their minds use the silence as they wish. Or you can suggest ways they might use the silence. For example,

- Practice abdominal breathing (introduced in Unit 2)
- Simply pay attention to your breathing
- Pay attention to sounds you hear in your mind, take yourself to a peaceful place
- Recall a time you had fun
- Recall something you like to do

After the time of silence, ask for a couple of volunteers to share where their minds went during the time. Make time for silence every day, preferably at the same time, such as after lunch or recess or the first and last actions of the day.

By giving students the opportunity to experience time for silence on a daily basis, you'll be instilling a habit that will serve them well for the rest of their lives.

Consider having your students keep a 4Rs journal

Writing (drawing for younger students) is an excellent way to reinforce and consolidate learning. A journal enables students to put all of their Book Talk writing in one place. You can also give them a few minutes after each 4Rs lesson to jot down a few thoughts about what they're taking away or how they're planning to use what they've just learned. If a student tries a new skill, s/he might want to write about what happened. Did it bring a positive result? If a student is stuck in a conflict with someone, s/he might want to do some writing to sort it out and imagine some solutions. You can give them standard journals and encourage them to decorate them.

By having students keep journals, you will be introducing them to a habit or practice that can serve them well the rest of their lives.

Class meetings for problem solving

In this kind of class meeting the teacher empowers students, facilitating a process by which students apply the skills they're developing through 4Rs lessons to real-life situations in the classroom and the school. By the time you reach Unit 5, your students should have the foundational skills (managing feelings, listening, assertiveness) to be good problem solvers. Also, Unit 5 introduces the ABCDE problem-solving model, an approach children can easily grasp. A free downloadable copy of Morningside Center's comprehensive guide, *Class Meetings for Problem Solving*, is available by request.

Related Books

The Bracelet by Yoshiko Uchida, Joanna Yarley, illus.
The Children of Topaz: The Story of a Japanese-American Internment Camp Based on a Classroom Diary by Michael O. Tonnell, George W. Chilcoat
Passage to Freedom: The Sugihara Story by Ken Mochizuki, Dom Lee, illus.
So Far from the Sea by Eve Bunting, Chris Sontpiet, illus.
Teammates by Peter Golenbock, illustrated by Paul Bacon

Handout 1 • Unit 7

Overview of The 4Rs™ for Grade 3

	Theme	Story
Unit 1	Building Community: Creating a Vision	Stone Soup
Unit 2	Feelings	JoJo's Flying Side Kick
Unit 3	Listening	The Pain and the Great One
Unit 4	Assertiveness	Hank Aaron: Brave in Every way
Unit 5	Problem Solving	Old Henry
Unit 6	Diversity / Countering Bullying	One
Unit 7	Making a Difference	Baseball Saved Us

Grade 3 — Baseball Saved Us

Handout 2 • Unit 7

My Gift for the World

Name_____ Class_____ Date_____

School_____

City_____ State_____

I pledge to _____

_____

_____

Here's what it might look like

Bibliography

Works cited in The 4Rs: activities adapted from or permission given for use.

Derman-Sparks, Louise, *Anti-Bias Curriculum: Tools for Empowering Young Children*. National Association for the Education of Young Children, Washington, D.C. 1989.

Kreidler, William J., *Conflict Resolution in the Middle School: A Curriculum and Teacher's Guide*. esr / Educators for Social Responsibility, Cambridge, MA. 1994.

Kreidler, William J., *Creative Conflict Resolution: More Than 200 Activities for Keeping Peace in the Classroom K-6*. Good Year Books / Scott, Foresman and Company, Glenview, Illinois. 1984.

Kreidler, William J., *Elementary Perspectives: A Teaching Guide to Concepts of Peace*. ESR, Cambridge, MA. 1990.

Kreidler, William J., *Teaching Conflict Resolution Through Children's Literature, Grades K-2*. Scholastic Professional Books, New York. 1994.

Kreidler, William J. and Lisa Furlong, *Adventures in Peacemaking: A Conflict Resolution Activity Guide for School-age Programs*. Project Adventure. 1995.

Kreidler, William J. and Sandy Tsubokawa Whittall, *Early Childhood Adventures in Peacemaking*, 2nd edition. ESR, Cambridge, MA. 1999.

Prutzman, Priscilla et al, *The Friendly Classroom for a Small Planet*. New Society Publishers, Gabriola Island, BC, Canada, 1988. © Children's Creative Response to Conflict, P.O. Box 271, Nyack, NY 10960. Tel. (845) 353-1796.

Ray, Peggy and Sheila Alson, Linda Lantieri, and Tom Roderick, *Resolving Conflict Creatively: A Teaching Guide for Grades Kindergarten Through Six*. Board of Education of the City of New York, New York. 1993, 1996.

Schneidewind, Nancy and Ellen Davidson, *Open Minds to Equality*, 2nd ed. Allyn and Bacon, Needham Heights, MA. © 1998.

Teaching Tolerance, publication of the Southern Poverty Law Center, Spring 1999, p. 48 (Grade 1, p.86)

Weiss, Evelyn, ed., Priscilla Prutzman, Nancy Silber, *Children's Songs for a Friendly Planet*. World Around Songs, Inc., 1986.

York, Stacey, *Roots & Wings: Affirming Culture in Early Childhood Programs*. Redleaf Press / a division of Resources for Child Caring, St. Paul, MN. 1991.

Index of Activities, Closings, Gatherings, & Handouts

Activities

ABCDE Approach to Problem Solving	95
Abdominal breathing	33
Active Listening: the 3 Ps	52
• 1st: Pay Good Attention	53
• 2nd: Provide gentle encouragement	54
• 3rd: Paraphrase	55
Assertiveness Line	77
Balancing	96
Brainstorm solutions (A**B**CDE)	95
Bullying Web	107
Choices (Assertive Role-play)	71
Completing our pledges	135
Conflict: Introducing the Concept	56
Conflict: Review definition	90
Conflict Web	57
Consequences (Role-play)	74
Creative Conflict Solving	93
Dealing with Bullying	115
Draining	76
Exploring what happens when we have a strong feeling	26
Face to Face	109
Family Banners	111
Feelings Barometer	26
Feelings, Stories about	25
Feelings Web	24
Gift I can give the world [pledge]	133
Good and Poor Listening	9
Have A Heart	11
Have A Heart Story	12
Introductory Note to the Teacher (about Choices)	70
I-Messages	75
It's not fair!	112
Mashed Potatoes	24
Mirroring	24
Plan 1-2-3	35
Point of view [role-play]	59
Prejudice and Discrimination	112
Presenting our pledges/getting support	136
Problem Solving: ABCDE approach	95
Put-Ups and Put-Downs	11
Quick Thinking (Standing up…)	113
Reflecting on our year with The 4Rs	131
Reporting vs Tattling	118
Role-play (point of view)	59
Roles in Bullying Situations	102
Self-talk	32
Strong, Mean, and Giving In	73
Things Bullies Do	116
Think Differently	10, 117
Time I Felt Different, A	109
Triggers: fear, nervousness, anger	29
Vision of Classroom Community	8
Ways we deal with fear, nervousness, anger	30
What we can do (re bullying)	117
Win-Win Solutions	90
Writing about conflict	57

Additional Activities

Class Meeting for Problem Solving	97, 119, 137
Cloudy and Clear	37
Conflict Escalator	61
Creating a Peace Corner	39
Drawing a Peaceful Place	38
Hillel the Wise	13
Keep a 4Rs Journal	13, 40, 62, 79, 97, 119, 137
Make time for silence	13, 39, 61, 79, 96, 119, 136
Other Situations (Assertiveness Role-play)	78
Peace Corner	39
Strong Message Machine	79
What is peace?	38
Who's Missing?	61

Closings

ABCDE Cheer	96
Applause	37, 73, 114
Balancing	118
Connections	76
Doing Something I Enjoyed	74
Group Hug	136
High Five	9, 111
How I feel right now	25
Moment of Silence	54
New Millennium Telephone Game	56
Pass the Sound	10, 78
Pausing to breathe	34
Quick, quick, slow	94
Rhythm	132
Someone I Appreciate	12, 126
Something I'm looking forward to	61, 116
Something I'm thankful for	110
Song: I Whistle a Happy Tune	31
Song: There Is Always Something You Can Do	92
Stretches	58
Tree in a storm	134
What I can do to improve my mood	28

When I can use abdominal breathing 34

Gatherings

Alphabet Soup 94
Attribute Linking 108
Ballooning 31
Birthday Line Up 131
Changes 56
Clap and repeat 55
Cooper Says 9
Count to Five 89
Deep Breathing 115
Freeze 73
Freeze 2 75
Go-Round: Intro to practice 52
Louder/Softer 58,76
Mirroring 11
Name Game 8,23
Rainstorm 132
Someone I'm grateful for 135
Something I enjoy w/my family 110
Song: If You're Happy 25
Squeeze-Relax 29
Stand Up 92
A Strong Wind Blows 71
This Is a [Balloon] 112

Time I helped someone 116

Charts, Handouts, Song Sheets, & Webs

Chart: Stop, Think, Breathe 35
Chart: Triggers for Fear, Nervousness, Anger 29
Chart: Ways Conflicts Can Turn Out ... 91
Chart: Ways we deal with things that
freak us out 30
Handout: ABCDE Problem Solving Method 99
Handout: Heart Pattern 15
Handout: Hillel the Wise 16
Handout: I-Message Form 81
Handout: "My Gift for the World" 139
Handout: Overview of The 4Rs 138
Handout: Script for Bullying Skit 121
Handout: Triggers & Self-talk 43
Song Sheet: I Whistle A Happy Tune .. 42
Song Sheet: If You're Happy 41
Song Sheet: There Is Always Something
   You Can Do 98
Tips for Teachers re The 4Rs xiii
Web: Bullying 107
Web: Conflict 57
Web: Feelings 24